PRAISE FOR WHA

Once again Jack Remick has pr rs with his passionate choice of w is new work, *What Do I Know? W* ...ssays. He is a man of many words and offers his readers the gift of learning how to express their feelings with less fear of discovering who they are. Jack is my friend as well as coach. I admire his commitment to his craft and for the art of spectacular storytelling abilities that he shares with all of us.
—**Marsha Cook**, Michigan Avenue Media Inc.

The intensity and depth of Jack Remick's reflections on wisdom go beyond brilliant, original, mind-bending. The searching questions in these essays are quintessential to our fraught times and they set off my own convoluted thoughts about wisdom—what is it? Do I have it? *What Do I Know?* is one of those books that will be read and reread, discussed, thought over, and read again. Its lucidity will reverberate.
—**Priscilla Long**, author *of Fire and Stone: Where Do We Come From? What Are We? Where Are We Going?*

In these essays Jack Remick explores the various arts and many sciences, romps across historical eras, and invokes writers and thinkers from Marcus Aurelius to Mao. *What Do I Know?* never tires of asking provocative questions, and entertaining difficult ideas. At the core of these essays are the notions of obsolescence, irrelevance and redundancy, and to navigate, he invents a brand new word, *irredundancy*. Remick wears his decades well, and his inquiries will spark lively response from any thoughtful reader.
—**Laura Kalpakian**, author of *Memory Into Memoir*

Jack Remick dives deep into the bones, the blood, the beating heart of the human experience. These essays are not light musings—they are life examined with the attention of the scholar, the precision of the surgeon, and the passionate angst of the poet.
—**Jessica H. Stone**, author of *Blook on a Blue Moon*

"Without our history, are we even here? We are not as wise as birds because we have to ask the questions—where have we come from? Where are we going? We are the only species that cannot just be." With humility and provocative summation of insight gleaned across the lifespan of his numerous published works, poet and author Jack Remick's *What Do I Know? Wisdom Essays* embodies a seminal inquiry by an anguished, always eloquent, and brilliant intellect. The work strikes an open and unflinching conversation with the reader, equivalent in the authority and illumined perspicacity to the meditations of Marcus Aurelius (A.D. 121-180) and Blaise Pascal (1623-1662) centuries earlier. And therein lies the enlightened paradox of this collection: *"In the end, at the finish, the writer has to ask—is it done? Is this ending the last ending? Is there a forever? The answer to that is, of course, no. No is the finish. Niente. Nada. Nihil. Nothing."* Remick's probing quest, *What Do I Know?,* liberates meaning for those lives of contemporaneous readers where no answers are available.
—**Dennis Must**, author of *Brother Carnival, Hush Now, Don't Explain, The World's Smallest Bible, Going Dark, Oh, Don't Ask Why*

WHAT DO I KNOW?

WISDOM ESSAYS

JACK REMICK

WHAT DO I KNOW?

WISDOM ESSAYS

JACK REMICK

Sidekick Press
Bellingham, Washington

Published 2021
Printed in the United States of America
ISBN: 978-0-9914258-9-1 (hardcover) | 978-0-9914258-8-4 (paperback)
LCCN: 2021940500

Sidekick Press
2950 Newmarket Street, Suite 101-329
Bellingham, Washington 98226
sidekickpress.com

Jack Remick, *What Do I Know? Wisdom Essays*
Author photo ©2020 by Anne Herman
Cover design ©2021 by Meredith Bricken Mills and Spoken Design

"The Wisdom of Tools: The Mason" originally printed in *So Much Depends Upon…*
"The Arrogance of the Princely Mind" originally printed in *Raven Chronicles, Volume 26: Last Call*
"The Wisdom of Finishing" originally printed in *Raven Chronicles, Volume 26: Last Call*
"The Wisdom of Marriage" originally printed in *Feminine Collective* (online review, ed. Julie Anderson)
"The Wisdom of Women" originally printed in *Bhubaneswar Review* (online review in Bhubaneswar, India)

DEDICATION

These essays are dedicated to those who died from this plague, to those who survived the pandemic, and to those who survived and yet know they will never return to normal. The "Covid body" is a fragmented one; the "Covid mind" is a reminder of what we once were.

I cannot name all the writers I have worked with over the years, writers who helped me become a better writer. I wrote these essays at the now closed Louisa's Café Bakery and Bar in Seattle, where many novelists and poets created their art. When Luise and Michael Mooney sold the café, life changed, but the art did not. Together we found ways to unleash the mysteries of the mind.

Special thanks to Jessica H. Stone and to Eleanor Parker Sapia, serious writers who worked with me through the pandemic years to produce their wonderful novels and delightful poetry while holding me to a high standard of storytelling and language use.

Dennis Must, who is "My Brother in Words," read drafts of these essays and with his late-style mind and eye showed me how to write beyond myself so that the words resonated deeper and reached further than they would have without his guidance.

I am indebted to Catherine Treadgold for editing this book. Without her experience and expertise, I would have destroyed English syntax with my idiosyncratic style. Catherine lets no word through without serious scrutiny. She taught me that a writer's best friend is not the computer but the dictionary.

To Helen, who is not a guide but my conscience.

CONTENTS

WISE [ADJ.]

Old English *wis* "learned, sagacious, cunning; sane; prudent, discreet; experienced; having the power of discerning and judging rightly," from Proto-Germanic **wissaz* (source also of Old Saxon, Old Frisian *wis*, Old Norse *viss*, Dutch *wijs*, German *weise* "wise"), from past-participle adjective **wittos* of PIE root *weid*—"to see" (hence "to know"). Modern slang meaning "aware, cunning" first attested 1896. Related to the source of Old English *witan* "to know, wit." (source: Online Etymology Dictionary)

A wise man has no extensive knowledge;
He who has extensive knowledge is not a wise man.
—[Lao Tzu, *Tao Te Ching*, c. 550 BCE]

JANUARY 5

WISDOM IN THE TWENTY-FIRST CENTURY

Irredundant—a portmanteau word for the relative position of a man at seventy-four in a culture gone mad. Redundant married to irrelevant.

How is it that today not much is left of the Enlightenment worldview of those who wrote the Constitution—those who built the wall between Church and State? Those who said that the separation of powers is the foundation of a wise and just government?

Supreme Court justices now say that black men are inferior to white men. They say that Christianity is God's religion. They say that all other religions are fake. I ask myself—is that wise?

I have been writing about wisdom and its ramifications, but as I look around, I ask myself: why is there so little wisdom left?

Perhaps it's because we don't know what wisdom is. What is it? How do we get it? Can we borrow it? Are we born with it?

In these essays, I wish to explore wisdom with an end in mind: finding answers to the questions that have long hounded me. Am I wise? Have I ever been wise? Can I ever be wise? What happens to wisdom when the mind dies its living death of Forget?

When I was young, I thought marriage was irrelevant. I thought that marriage was not necessary. I have been married for fifty-three years to a woman I admire and love, a woman I consider my best friend. Is that a stupid thing to say? Yes. I am human. I want to be wise.

I'm married to a woman who seems to have been born wise. She knows and understands political ideas I struggle to comprehend. Trial and error guide me to places where she already lives, and shines, and her light fills the space around her.

Into this perfection, what do I bring?

A load of gonadal, male, testosterone-driven nonsense.

The woman I married never stands still. She transcends evolutionary restraints and lives in an age of enlightenment that both shocks and amazes me.

From her, for example, I have learned the value of silence. The value of quiet, the way of the Tao from a woman who has a PhD in Psychology and is a quilter of international stature as well as a national authority on women's rights and comparable worth.

From her, I learned that while men as mechanics and tunnel rats and sanitation specialists work dirty jobs, women as nurses work in human filth—piss and the pissed pants of the sick, the shit-filled diapers of the old, mouthfuls of vomit from the near dead. She told me that one of her interview subjects described in detail the moment when she was giving CPR to a heart attack victim who vomited in her mouth. That is what I learned from this woman.

Men fight and kill. We are whiners and babies and malingerers while it's women who keep the world on its pivot.

She taught me to go beyond my maleness and its evolutionary load to get to a place beyond the physical—and in so doing she pointed me to the space beyond religion, beyond spirituality. A place of quiet stillness, the zone of indifference saturated with a sense of duty.

Though not religious, my wife is moral. Her example tells me that morality and religion are not linked. She does not kill but has no link to any of the Judeo-Christian biblical lore. She sees the absolute absurdity of religion when it ceases to be private and becomes a public, political, ping-pong ball. Belief is not fact. Belief should stay in its place. The fact that belief has no place in public policy might be the essence of all wisdom.

And from her I learned the integrity of enlightenment married to compassion for us, the pitiable race, the lone survivors, the last hairless apes. From her I learned respect for the children who are brought unthinking into a world of thieves and terrorists, a world of cheaters, of killers, and polluters. She has taught me to respect the child and to teach the child.

But what do we teach the child?

A lawyer I once met worked with the Chinese to set up a system of laws for the post-Maoist state. She asked the question—"If you don't fall back on religion, what do you base a legal system on?"

In China, religion was Confucian, but Confucianism was in and of itself a system of ethics, not legalism. So, what do you teach the child?

The questions remain: Where is wisdom? How do we get it?

Where does wisdom enter the educational system? How do you define right and wrong if you don't have a basis in authority?

We do not know, so we fall back on some existential base of priority—e.g., *do not take what does not belong to you*—but how do you know what belongs to whom?

In an essay on the Strongman, I wrote that the Strongman hates the law because it strips him of his perceived entitlement that might makes right. In the past, the Strongman took what he wanted because he was strong. I concluded that the Strongman who hates law written and enforced by weaker men, hates even more the idea of a female police force. To the Strongman, that is the ultimate contradiction—a female cop enforcing the law of the weak many to constrain the Strongman who will not take orders from a woman. We see this acted out every day now—men rebel, and in rebelling act as if they are strong and can take possession of whatever they want.

How do we teach children to reject might over justice?

What do we tell them?

Do we tell them to kick the snot out of their enemies?

Is that wisdom?

Do we tell them to kill the people who don't agree with them?

Is that wise?

Murder the weak because they don't deserve to breathe the same air as the strong?

That is Donald Trump. That is Antonin Scalia. That is Vladimir Putin. That is Amy Coney Barrett. They are anachronisms living in an ancient, unevolved world full of hate and hurt and stupidity, a world driven by belief.

They might as well be carrying clubs and throwing stones and wearing animal skins.

Is that what we teach the child?

Is compassion a weakness? Is law a weakness? When we lived in huts or in caves, when we lived in tents or sod houses, there was not much need for law—but when we reach eight billion bodies worldwide, we need rules for behavior.

We can't allow the strong to simply take what they want—but that is what we do.

We should, instead of killing, admire those who have passed through rituals, survived the fires, endured famine and plague. We should celebrate their achievements, and the way to celebrate is to find rules that will guide us.

Once rules are written, how do we enforce them?

How do we confront the issue of symbols?

A female cop can be overwhelmed by a strong man. Swift, in *Gulliver's Travels*, shows us the power of the many working in concert—the many, weak as we are, can tie the giant to stakes and nail his hands to the floor and gut him—but only if we work together.

The common mistake is to think that it is the strong competitor who wins, when in fact, the real winner is the one who cooperates. In this time of illness, of fascism, or kleptocratic politics, we forget that—trapped in the last restraints of the evolutionary process—we live by what we know as *residual evolutionary responses*. We bring Paleolithic reactions to Atomic-Age stimuli. What worked ten thousand years ago does not work when MAD (mutual assured destruction) is possible. One turn of the key and we are no more.

Without enlightenment, hundreds of Nagasakis and thousands of Hiroshimas are on the horizon. Without wisdom and without more women like the woman I have been married to for fifty-three years, the horrors will continue.

But I have to ask: Why do women allow the strong and the stupid to rule? Why do women vote for a Republican for any office at any time, in any jurisdiction, knowing that the

Republican agenda is a religio-fascist, repressive one? Why do women vote for a Republican, knowing that the Republican agenda is aimed at controlling a woman's freedom to choose? In the United States, a hundred years ago, women fought for the right to vote. Now, using that vote, so many women choose to enslave themselves in the capitalist-fascist-religious matrix.

Women have not escaped the past. Just as men do, women bring with them the past, and in our minds, there is a residue of the Paleolithic. We have to live with that residue or perish because of it.

Wisdom. What is it? How do we get it?

THE WISDOM OF REMEMBERING

As I write this, I am seventy-five. Because I'm seventy-five, I ought to have by now at least a touch of wisdom, but as I look at myself in the mirror of the universe, I see that I am irrelevant, redundant, and infinitesimally significant.

I am neither big nor small.

I am neither brilliant nor dull.

This question of irrelevance and its relation to wisdom bothers me. There are things I ought to be able to tell others, but what I know seems to have no relevance beyond my knowing it. Maybe wisdom is knowing that you are irrelevant and the evolved ego is an anachronism telling us we should have become social insects.

But the ego prevents us, prevents *me*, from measuring my insignificance and in fact insists on placing me—the servant of my ego—at the center of all things. I call this the *egosphere.*

Maybe, then, wisdom is learning how to avoid this raging beast that lives somewhere in my mind and screams *me, me, me, me*—never *us*, never *all of us*, but *me, me, me*.

In the '60s, we dreamed psychedelic—the posters were nonlinear, the writing was nonlinear, the music was nonlinear. It was a dreaming life in a time of insignificance, and now, fifty years into our time of death, psychedelia just might give me a clue to the meaning of wisdom.

When my wife and I had a child, we knew she was an evolutionary, biological trick played on us by our genes, by the system into which we had evolved. Even then, knowing that, we could not quiet the parts of us that carried the love out into the open. Maybe wisdom isn't consciousness at all. Maybe wisdom is the result of acceding to the inevitable residual evolutionary responses we call love, anger, fear, need, and greed.

All of these pre-Paleolithic constructs are the past living in our egos—in my ego—in the present, and I am trying to fashion an atomic vision of living using tools that evolved to produce stone objects. I am one of those who thinks he has an emotional, psychical, cerebral set of tools that have fallen behind his other technological truths.

So how can wisdom proceed from an ancient set of ideas born into my body through no choice of my own? Maybe wisdom is knowing how to choose rather than react, but right now every decision, while seeming to be mine, is actually the residual action repeated through time by those who came before me.

They bequeathed their Paleolithic art and arsenals to me, leaving me to live in a fantasy world of choice and decision. All the while the finger on the trigger resembles nothing but a stone.

We have turned stone to steel, turned the sling into a rifle, and we project, *I* project, said transformed stone into the gut or brain of another animal, another human. We kill.

I know that it was not the competitive one whose tools—read "our RERs"—came down to me, but the cooperative one whose wolf sense told him, "work together."

Still, in the brain, somewhere in the brain, there is a mind, and in the mind there is a construct called ego, the ego that comes along for the ride and shatters the tools of cooperation and turns them into weapons intended for killing.

Maybe wisdom isn't knowing how to kill, but when.

This divide between what and when has bothered me for a long time. Is it wisdom not to tell anybody anything if in fact the sole purpose of the ego is to create the world an infinite number of times?

Years ago, I broke in working underground in tunnels in South America with my father. He was a man who organized vast construction projects involving thousands of men, and he made it all work to produce the desired and coveted end—on time and under budget.

I asked him one day why he didn't write a book. He told me he was taking everything he knew to the grave—leaving none of it. Not one word—except the knowledge he had given to other men—and that knowledge involved not just knowing what to do but when to do it.

This split, then, between *what* and *when* is somehow at the core of wisdom, but in my father, wisdom was not a gift but a practice.

When the time came that he could no longer practice what he knew, he did not care. Wisdom is in the doing, and learning is in the watching how it's done. Wisdom is the practice of the What along with the When, but added to this is something just as important—the Why.

It is the Why that gives the When its luster and its value. The Why tells me when to plant—so the seed reaches fullness at a certain time—and what to do to make that happen. Why, What, When must be the residue or the substance of wisdom.

When I teach writing, I tell writers to write the ending of the story first. Why? To set a limit.

No story can be open-ended because there are conventions to story. Imagine, for example, the raconteur, sitting around the campfire, sees into the mind of the listener and charts the path through the darkness. In the darkness, there is fear—another residual evolutionary response—fear of the night, of the silence, of the predator. For the raconteur, the ending has to be in the light; it has to be in the hope of life. When? The raconteur knows the end before the story begins, so in the telling, the storyteller lays out a map that the listener takes in, and along the way, the storyteller drops hints of how the story will end—hinting, although the listener doesn't know it, at the myth already in the mind of the listener.

I imagine a time in the dark when the stone-point maker mapped out the hunt and in the telling taught the young how to do it. The end is the meat. The Why is to eat. The When is in the light. The What is the method.

Now, however, Wisdom is fragmented and the mind created by our evolved responses is lost in the new time. Therefore, wisdom has no name.

No one comes to ask me How.

No one asks me What.

No one asks me When.

There is no When, there is no Why, because in the time of fragmentation the mind is still evolving, trying to catch up in its behavior to what its practiced abstract essence has created. How can a mind evolved to hurl stones at fifty miles per hour ever understand the truth of a missile traveling at three thousand miles per hour?

This is the bottleneck in wisdom. The Paleolithic past lives in the fingertips and in the trigger finger, but the What has shifted from the hunt to the killing and no longer focuses on the Why.

What is wisdom in the Anthropocene?

It is nothing because pace of invention outstrips rate of memory. What I know now has no use for a writer evolving in the future. There is nothing I can pass on—just as my father, in his wisdom, knew that his knowledge was passé even before he died. And he was right. In a way.

In New Mexico, I ran a tunnel-boring machine called a Robbins mole. At that time, it was customary to drill rock and blast it with dynamite. The mole, by contrast, is a brute-force machine that grinds stone into fine powder.

Now, as material science creates new devices, even the Robbins mole has been dwarfed by huge machines working at a faster pace than ever imagined in the drill-and-shoot world.

Anything any man knew about the latter is dated, passé, useless. That is the fate of wisdom. It is not eternal, but temporal. It is not creative but categorical.

Wisdom lost is never to be found again, and so my father was wise in a way by taking what he knew to his grave. He gave way to the creatures of the new way, just as the stone-point maker gave way to the bullet and the hunter gave way to the murderer.

It gives me a lot to think about—the killing, and how easily it can be done.

Why?

What?

When?

The three elements of true wisdom, now fading fast in a world still in creation.

JANUARY 12

THE WISDOM OF BABY FAT

At night, as I wait for sleep, my brain is alight from the hours of reading.

In my poem, "The Painted Interior," I asked—am I more than meat and bone? Am I more than flesh or stone? I wrote it, but don't have any idea what it means. As I sit here now writing this, I ask if anything we do, I do, you do, is nothing more than *a residual evolutionary response*?

What is in an RER?

If I call the RER instinct, I get flak from those who see the Anthropocene as the ultimate goal of evolution.

In his book, *Brain Architecture*, Larry Swanson writes that the cerebral cortex is the crowning achievement of evolution.

But the cerebral cortex evolved from older brains and in those brains we find the apparatus that triggers the RER.

We do not will our heart to beat; we do not will our lungs to breathe. Our control of the reflexes is nil. Our immune system works without conscious effort. The man does not will his sperm into existence, the woman does not will her ova to the follicles. Our brains operate twenty-four hours a day, seven days a week, three hundred sixty-five days a year until we die.

But what is the tissue that makes us think? The cerebral cortex. What is it that makes us breathe? The cerebellum. What makes us feel? The limbic brain. All of it up to the cerebral cortex is the result of natural selection, and without the three brains, we are not. And there is no god.

I see a young woman. Her body fat is at twenty-two percent. Her skin is smooth. Her teeth are white. Her eyes are clear. I see a perfect outcome. A woman resulting from three million years of natural selection. Why do I look at her?

I'm past reproductive age. I have already engendered an offspring who has produced offspring—but still I look. Why?

RER. Built into the body is the natural wisdom that lays out the natural plan and no man, no woman, is exempt. Each of us is the sum of our primitive brain, our mid-brain, and the cerebral cortex. We are, in fact, creatures of our brains.

I look at this young, ripe, full-bodied woman, but I know that at this moment I am irrelevant. Not just to her, but to the course of evolution itself. So, what am I in old age? I am not that old man with bad breath who, forgetting that his testes long ago dried into desiccated residual ridiculousness, leches after the young woman who, driven as she is by her own RERs, laughs at him and his foul breath.

Old age is the time of physical redundancy—and the wisdom to recognize it keeps me from making a fool of myself. And only that wisdom—the wisdom of knowing what *not* to do.

Wisdom is, in a sense, then, the cerebral cortex with its thinking apparatus running full tilt and overriding the RER. And there are so many of these responses.

An ocean of being rests under the crowning achievement—I am evolved. What I do and say is no more creative than a snake tracking a frog. Everything is an extension of firsts. Houses are extensions of the cave. The fork is an extension of the finger. Chopsticks are an extension of the bone. What we bring is always cloaked in what has already been. The bow is an extension of the arm, the bullet an extension of the arrow. The rocket an extension of the bullet.

We grow the future using the meat of the past. The RER is the First of Firsts that gives us pause as the cerebral cortex analyzes the process and allows or disallows it.

Yes, ask her the question. No, do not ask her the question. The residue of the past is lodged in the synapses of the limbic brain. Your eyes dilate in the dark. Your pupils contract in the sunlight and there's nothing you can do about it. You swallow because the cerebellum controls the flow of saliva in your mouth. The saliva comes at the thought of food and you react as all animals react in the presence of food—your stomach churns, peristalsis causes your bowels to move, and there's nothing you can do about it. RER.

When consciousness relents, the sea-deep mind speaks—Jack Moodey wrote those words as he sat in the shade of a jasmine tree. He wrote it with a pen on paper, and that is a wonder. The cerebral cortex takes the signs and decodes them into meaning. But the first signs were tracks of animals in the sand. RER.

Now, back to irrelevance.

Wisdom. I think. I write. Here, my cerebral cortex is working, guiding the pen as it pulls words out of a lexicon buried in my brain. Where are those words? How do they explode from the cerebral cortex back into signs on the page that I can write as if they all reside side-by-side, astonishing and real, and forever? How is that possible?

The brain is the governor. The cerebral cortex is the traffic cop. The signs are warnings and readings of space and time and the governor says "do not speak." What is the cerebral cortex measuring?

I don't know, but I do know that often I am silent when before I would have spoken. Wisdom now is knowing when not to speak. But what is being measured? And how does the cerebral cortex measure it?

I used to process current affairs and get angry—what? Why? There is nothing I can do to sway the direction of cultural discourse—RER. That anger tempts me to say I have an answer—but I do not and now I *know* that I do not.

How is *that* measure taken?

Does my cerebral cortex know more than I do?

Does my limbic brain know more than I do?

How can I answer? Now, I know when not to go past the edge of the abyss—wherever it is—the measure is taken—perhaps weighing time and distance against lost sleep and comfort.

I don't ask the young woman the question because I don't want to make a fool of myself. Wisdom?

Is that a residual evolutionary response?

I ask—what would I see if I went on a trip? What would I do? Where would I sleep? What would I eat?

The cerebral cortex overrides the limbic brain and the cerebellum, both of which dictate movement into space. As they keep my balance, taking readings from cilia in my inner ears and reporting to the cerebral cortex on the condition of the body in time and space, there is, of course, a deeper question: Why do you want to go there? The answer to that question eventually leads us either to the top of the mountain or to Mars. We are travelers because of the RERs that drove us out of our caves because we had to get somewhere else. In our nomadic past, rarely was being *here* enough. We are all unmoored, each in a personal way, and we are all looking for a pathway to a future that will save us.

Somewhere in the limbic brain, a synapse tells me to keep moving. If you are moving, you will find food, you will find a mate, you will find a hole to climb into for shelter and protection. RER. Everything I do—from the words on this page to the hunger pang in my gut—is an extension of the first brain carrying over into the Now. The Now is our trouble spot.

In the Now, there are so many of us. All reacting to the need to be together and clustered in one spot, we bring our spatial quest to bear, and we kill.

We kill those who do not look like us, all the while cooperating in the killing with others who are like us. We kill those who do not believe what we believe, all the while killing in tandem with those believers who believe like us.

Even the killing is an RER.

Difference is the trigger.

Death is the stone.

Ego is the map that guides us into needing others like ourselves.

Ego is the trap that guides us into an extension of ourselves, and in ourselves we see the result of sameness. The cerebral cortex does not admit difference, but why does it allow difference to exist? RER.

The cerebral cortex itself is the RER in the sweep of competition, in the body of the young woman with the baby fat at twenty-two percent and dark skin silky as warm oil.

The cerebral cortex has to be the ultimate heir to the treasure in the limbic brain.

And the cerebellum—it cannot exist alone—relies on the primal RER for its existence. Where in the brain does the mind hide?

I erred in ever thinking that I was relevant, and that is the result of ego, which does not reside in the brain but is a product of the mind, which is a product of the brain. And there is nothing I can do to change this reality.

All of it is illusion. The meaning of my existence, the lack of meaning to my existence, the fear of death—an RER that forces us to jerk at the first jab of the spear point, to cringe at the first threat of a bullet.

I am irrelevant, and irrelevance is a state of being I inherited the moment I first emerged.

JANUARY 15

THE WRITING GODS

Every day when I'm working, I look up at least once expecting to see an aura, a ray of light bringing me wisdom. But then I go back to the page, back to the words, back to the story. What does wisdom mean to me as a writer and to the characters I write about, whose stories I tell? Not sure yet.

A while ago, after hearing Junot Diaz talk at the library, I wrote a piece about women and their writing gods. The pain you see in an audience of women as a star shines is real, ageless, and permanent. The Writing God stands at the podium hurling bolts of fire at the breathless audience, and in the words, there is a peculiar wisdom that oozes out over the hurting ones—"this is life," the words ring out, "this is pain. This is how it's done, this is your god of writing talking"—and in the talk there is a healing of the wounds, a sealing of the word wounds, and the women walk away feeling light and free . . . until they get home. Then the light shining from the god fades and the darkness descends again and the lame are lame again and the hurt are hurting again and the pained ones are in jeopardy again, one step from the razor's edge. Not even The Writing God can assuage the darkness of depression and the loss of self in this parlous time in the Anthropocene.

So, wisdom is either transitory and fading and waning or it is eternal and catholic.

I'm reading the *Meditations* of Marcus Aurelius at the same time I'm reading Dick Teresi's *Lost Discoveries: The Ancient Roots of Modern Science—from the Babylonians to the Maya.* Between the two I see a huge gulf. Wisdom has nothing to do with science. Science, as it waits for facts to emerge, is eternal and exists whether we acknowledge it or not. Science is in constant motion and change—except that, as with some of the *Meditations*, it persists.

Once a scientific truth is discovered, it persists. Copernicus used Sumerian and Babylonian math in his calculations to place the sun at the center of the planetary system.

But the Chinese had already by 200 BCE discovered that the Earth was round and the sun was the center of the solar system. Is that wisdom? I think not. That is science.

There is little science in the *Meditations*. There is a high degree of wisdom, if by wisdom I understand not only what to say but when to say it and its converse, what not to say. What not to say brings me to the question of love.

Love is independent of the beloved. The beloved is never locked to the lover. A woman can love her dog, a man can love his cat, boys and girls can love their bikes and their skateboards.

Using this word—love—as a loose connection of lover to beloved raises the question of the internal apparatus that unleashes love.

Love can be turned off. How is that possible? In a marriage, the successful lover knows exactly what not to say. It is as if the words that break the bonds are lurking in the demon-darkness but the lover never says the one thing, never says the breaking word that will rupture the bond, nor does the lover bring to light the faults of the loved one.

I am writing about the biology of desire. In my novel, *Citadel*, I asked the question: When and if you separate reproduction from desire, what is left? Did desire co-evolve with sex and reproduction to ensure projection into the future? Are we locked into biology forever? Perhaps not. In *A Crack in Creation*, Jennifer Doudna and Samuel Sternberg suggest that the entire human genome can be manipulated in such a way as to leave humans free from natural selection.

If you separate reproduction from desire, does desire still exist with the same power it had when reproduction was the biological imperative?

In *Citadel,* I create a world where men can no longer tell women what to do, a world where women totally control reproduction. Does desire run at the same pace when sex and sexuality are not linked to reproduction? Does desire even work without males? Certainly.

Is all wisdom connected to the biology of desire? And what is it? Desire? Lust? What drives lust? How much of *Meditations* is pointed at the deities? At god, which sometimes Marcus capitalizes and then at others sets in minuscule?

What remains of the core of the meditations if you strip out the deity? Does God even matter? Probably not. God has never mattered in the sweep of DNA and natural selection because the process exists beyond belief systems. There are only facts in natural selection and the facts project as eye color and melanin. Natural selection does not depend on a belief system.

Back to the link between wisdom and science.

Early science was used in the interest of the deity. Astronomy was not a pure science—say, as it became after Edwin Hubble—but a set of signs read out of the stars and linked to the priests who set the time for planting seeds. Wisdom was and still is knowing what to do and when to do it. Because the stars arrange themselves in clusters and because men named the clusters and by naming the clusters gained control of the future. Wisdom—what to do. Wisdom—when to do it. By controlling the future, priests learned how to reap and store grain so that in the downtime the others didn't starve. Rousseau was not a fan of iron and corn.

Science is at the foundation of civilization, and wisdom is knowing how to use science to predict and understand the future. Wisdom has something to do with time and the future.

In a marriage, the lover knows the effect of words on the loved one and so controls not just the self but also the future by knowing when not to say the ruinous words, "I think that you look . . ."

Linking the biology of desire that is a natural wisdom embedded in the body to the learned wisdom that is the domain of science, a person learns how to live not alone but in a group. What applies to the unit applies to the group. But how do you deal with variation?

Recombinant DNA produces variation, but it is uniformity that binds us into social groups, and in social groups, we find the means to our survival—the pair produces the triad and multiple triads produce the social unit and the biology of desire meets the collective wisdom when the lover chooses not to say to the loved one, "I think you are letting yourself go . . ." With that in mind, you can see the extrapolation into nations and people. By knowing what not to say, you can establish and keep an uneasy peace.

Wisdom has something to do with achieving peace in the self, and the self's relation to the other, and then the collective selves' relation to the collective others.

If it were otherwise, we would be dead. The subject of death brings me to another thought.

My son-in-law's father died on a Wednesday. He was a good person. He and his wife produced two sons. His sons produced three offspring. But now he is dead. Everything he told his sons died with him except those parts of his wisdom that they each chose to keep. He did not know that deep in each of his sons dwelled a woman. A woman who would choose to escape from the mind of the man in her.

Wisdom, then, has something to do with choice surviving death and living a long life. Wisdom is what you pass on to keep your offspring alive after you are not there to warn them away from the abyss.

Wisdom contains some aspect of perpetual life, but does all wisdom pass through eternity? How much of what I know is the residue of what others knew before me? Wisdom either has an eternal aspect that lets the past form me or it is only what I pull from experience that forms me.

In her book, *The Fragile Wisdom,* Grazyna Jasienska raises the question of natural wisdom, which she equates with a Darwinian/Lamarckian train of thought—the body knows what is best for the body, but the brain and its civilized constructs destroy the natural wisdom and we become fat.

Fat is a natural, necessary, fragile wisdom. But too much of it kills us and that is the essence of the fragile wisdom. Wisdom has something to do with walking the edge. Wisdom has something to do with facing extinction and not living in panic of it.

JANUARY 19

WISDOM AND IRREDUNDANCY

The same three questions, always the same three questions: What is wisdom? How do I get it? Why don't I have it? These three questions drive me to examine what I know and why what I know is now irrelevant in the world.

A fourth unspoken question has to be: Why do I want to be wise?

I feel time slipping away from me as I read obituaries. The diminishing—I now walk half the distance I used to walk, lift half the weight I used to lift. I get the feeling that everything I know is sliding deeper into irredundancy. This portmanteau word fits the situation. I spend a lifetime gathering and using, thinking and planning, and then one day, none of what I know means a thing to anyone around me.

This is the irredundant at maximum torque speeding toward oblivion, leaving all direction in chaos. I look now at books—new books, old books, French books, and English books, books in Spanish and Italian—and I am afraid that every word in them is obsolete, redundant, and irrelevant. Those three words—obsolete, irrelevant, and redundant—circumscribe my condition.

In *Meditations*, I see a book that has lasted two thousand years. It is a book that coaxes the reader to look at nature, to look at the transient nature of existence. *Meditations* teaches the reader not to seek fame and glory because they are transient—*sic transit Gloria mundi*—"thus passes worldly glory." Marcus writes about the folly of ego and desire, the folly of asking other men to validate your existence. Folly because, in a short time, they, too, will be dead, and in death, the ego needs no words of praise.

Is this wisdom? Does wisdom come to us or do we grasp for it? Possess it? Search it out? Steal it?

I look at my own work as it sits on the shelf of my room and I see nothing that will last. As a test I have been giving away books, and as I do, I ask myself, "why don't I feel any loss? What have I lost by giving away books?" Nothing. Each book had its moment of relevance, if only to me, its author, and other readers, but in the end, as the book falls into the garbage, what is lost? How many of us reread books? Novels? Books of facts? Why reread old books when every day the universe floods us with new ones? What are we looking for? *Nihil novi sub sole* ("There is nothing new under the sun.") Is the Writing God corrupt, leaving us with no reason at all to listen to him?

Is it possible to throw away wisdom? If I don't know what it is, how can I throw it away? So far in these essays, not essays so much as *pensées*, as Pascal used the term—thoughts, processes—in this set of *pensées*, I have written that wisdom is knowing what not to do, when not to utter the one word that destroys.

Wisdom is fragile. The brain, a three-pound organ, is in constant motion and renewal. A three-pound package that stores and retrieves vast quantities of information, facts, ideas, new ideas—but in one second, all that cache of ideas and thoughts, all that treasure vanishes. When the brain dies, all ends.

And so the question: Is wisdom the mind or the brain?

Mind is what brain does. You need only to think of sleep to see this truth. In sleep, there is no wisdom. Not one fact exists, not one idea escapes until the brain awakens and in the awakening resurrects mind.

The brain itself cannot be wise, but the mind in the brain might harbor all known wisdom for all time.

The mind is wise. At least it contains the clock that chimes—now you say this, now you do not. What meter governs the mind if in it there is a process that moderates the mind's will to be unfettered? We see this in logorrhea—when Wernicke's area in the brain is damaged and the tongue unleashes a verbal chaos. For the logorrheic, every word has its meaning but not one of them connects to another and out of context there is no meaning, only chaos.

This, we see, and in seeing, know that mind is what brain creates and when part of the brain dies, mind is damaged. Is that wisdom—recognizing the broken brain and the loss of mind?

The logorrheic has no monitor on the words, no meter for when and why and where. To the logorrheic, all words are equal and time is meaningless and so wisdom disconnects and all is lost.

Does wisdom reside in the words that Marcus Aurelius writes or does wisdom reside in the mind of the reader reading Marcus Aurelius? If a logorrheic read Marcus, would Marcus's wisdom settle into a chaotic brain to heal it? I don't know. Logorrhea—words without connection to other words. This suggests that context and connection are the parents and grandparents of meaning.

But, I don't know.

That is the wisest of all sentences—I do not know. It tells you that the mind is aware of what it is not. Is that wisdom? Knowing what you do not know? Is there wisdom in knowing you will never know?

As I read science and the history of science, I know there will be a time when I will not be and at that moment I cannot know the answers to such questions as, "will a human being ever set foot on Mars?" I don't know. "Is there agony in the final moment as I die, knowing I will never know?"

Is wisdom consciousness? Are all conscious beings wise?

Does the wolf's skill at killing the buffalo count as Wolf Wisdom? And the ants—so many ants—do they have Ant Wisdom? They do not have knowledge, although they sense what their chemical, hormonal trails should be and where they should go and they find their way back to the hill from the food source. Is human wisdom a construct of the mind as the mind is a construct of the brain? And what about the ants? What about the wolf? And the Steller's jays that bury their peanuts, their forage for winter, lost, if they forget. Is there a Steller's Jay Wisdom we have no knowledge of?

I don't know.

I need to know some things but I have no desire to know all things, although I do suspect that the brain, with enough time, could possess a knowledge of all things.

Maybe wisdom is being aware of the process of limitations.

My wife has no use for cosmology, while cosmology fascinates me. She knows what she needs to know and doesn't lament not knowing what she cannot.

She limits her knowledge without damaging who she is—she is as intact and pure and true at any moment of not knowing as she is in the lucid moment of knowing everything she knows, and knowing that, knows what she does not want to read or need to know. Is wisdom, then, *knowing*? That would suggest that wisdom is knowledge.

Or is wisdom nothing more than a summation and elimination of facts?

Perhaps wisdom is best left in the dark. This leads me to write about silence.

Silence to the speaking person is a choice. Choosing not to speak—even knowing that the outcome of another's action will be negative or harmful—might be wisdom, but is silence such as that moral or ethical?

Ethics do not stem from wisdom but from the collective action. Knowing what to do at a certain moment is the collective wisdom. "All humans are valuable" is an ethical thought with a finite extendibility. All humans are valuable. But are some more valuable than others?

What is lost if the Nazis kill Einstein in a broken world?

What is lost if Marie and Pierre Curie die before they discover radium?

What dies if Jennifer Doudna and Emmanuelle Charpentier remain silent about CRISPR?

Wisdom is transitional but not transgenerational, and that gets me back to irrelevance, redundancy, and obsolescence.

What I know can or cannot be transmitted transgenerationally, but the question has to be, "is my wisdom relevant to another generation?" Is it my "duty" to transmit, or, as with my father who told me he was "taking his knowledge to the grave," is death the logical end to all wisdom?

I read Marcus Aurelius to see what a man two thousand years ago had to say, and at the root of his wisdom is silence on the transient nature of being and a conscious awareness of the closeness and finality of death.

Whatever wisdom I possess that isn't of value to the next generation, whose task it is to find its temporal value, must die with me. *Meditations* has survived for two millennia because what Marcus saw and thought and wrote is either artifact or wisdom for all ages. But Marcus writes about god with a majuscule G and sometimes he writes about gods in minuscule and as soon as I read either of those words, I rebel. I rebel, because to me, in my finite wisdom, religion and its deities are an illness for which there is no cure.

Do those two words—god or gods—make everything in Marcus irrelevant and obsolete? Am I, a nonbeliever in a world of believers, wise for not following the wisdom of a man who did not know the current state of science and the size and scope of the universe?

I do not know what I don't know.

JANUARY 22

PRACTICAL AND STUPID WISDOM

Wisdom of rage.
Stupid rage.
Righteous anger.

In my quest to understand wisdom I bump up against a cluster of questions:

What is wisdom?
How do you get it?
How do you know you have it?
How do you know when you don't?
Is wisdom always useful?
Is there such a thing as impractical wisdom?
Is usefulness a special case for wisdom?
Is there a wisdom in rage?
Does the stupid person have a kind of stupid wisdom?
Does wisdom ever become obsolete?
Is there a temporal limit to wisdom?
Does wisdom run out with age?

It would seem that a person should become wiser with age but if I look around me I see that is not the case.

I also keep bumping up against god.

I continue reading *Meditations*, in which Marcus projects two constants—nature is everything, and in death, everything goes back into nature. In these constants, the stoic Marcus comes close to the notion of the preservation of mass and energy.

How did Marcus gain this wisdom?

And that brings us to the question of god.

Sometimes Marcus uses the word to suggest a monotheistic entity while at others he uses the plural, which suggests a kind of pagan residualism or a plurality of gods. I ask, is Marcus's wisdom temporally limited? One God. Many gods. Conservation of mass and energy means no soul. The question then of the temporal limitation of wisdom gets me back to the ideas of irrelevance, redundancy, and obsolescence.

Most of what I know—my "apparent" wisdom—is flying at light speed into obsolescence and irrelevance just as Marcus's plurality of gods has seen its time come and go. How do I separate the obviously arcane *belief* from the obviously physical *knowledge*?

I think that evolution is a timeless process that will not end. Descartes "believed"—here I have to set up the polarity: believe/think—that animals did not have souls, and he believed that in humans, the soul resided in the pineal gland.

This is the core of the puzzle: Is wisdom, with its temporal limitation, really wisdom, even in its own time?

Descartes was wrong—or was he? Whether or not he was wrong about animals not having souls had nothing to do with his geometric mind.

That wisdom—or *thought*—stands through time, and so, until it is proved not to apply, I have to accept it. But.

If a man's total wisdom is not intact, can I accept any aspect of it? At what point and in which part does Descartes lapse into irrelevancy and redundancy? Eric Kandel, in his early work, was eager to find the Freudian ego, id, or superego in the brain. He could not find them, and that failure launched him on a different route to understanding the brain. No one—no scientist, physiologist, or neurologist—can prove that the soul lives in the pineal gland. Do we reject all of Descartes or do we cherry-pick which parts of his wisdom to accept?

Marcus writes about time as he writes about death and fame. To Marcus's way of thinking, a man should live in his time and not try to live beyond it. That takes us back to the split between knowledge and wisdom.

To summarize: Wisdom is knowing what to do. Knowing when to do it. Knowing why to do it. When not to do it. In all these cases, wisdom and knowledge are equal. That leaves us with the unbearably complicated notion of impractical or stupid wisdom.

Impractical wisdom. Can there be such a thing—as in knowing that the knowing is of absolutely no use to animal or plant? Is that even possible? Can there be perfectly useless wisdom? Does wisdom imply usefulness? Example: my grandfather farmed a square mile of ground in Kansas. Before radio and the minute-to-minute weather report, he had a way to know when to plant the wheat. Did he inherit it—wisdom passing to him from an ancestor—or did he learn it by observation?

He was a farmer among other farmers. Did he learn when to harvest his wheat from them—acquired knowledge—or did he walk the fields and sample the wheat and decide from experience when it was time to harvest?

If my grandfather cuts that wheat in June instead of July, the wheat is bad. The harvest is no good. There is no bread.

Practical wisdom.

Wisdom seems to have at least two traits—practical and temporal.

Not one of my uncles now farms the ground my grandfather farmed, but when they lived with my grandfather, they all knew to the day when to plant, when to harvest, when to slaughter the hogs, when to sell the cattle at auction.

Is that wisdom gone? This brings me to temporality again and the question of residual wisdom: Wisdom that once was practical slides into obsolescence. A man working in an airplane factory—my uncle Kenneth—did not need to know anything about wheat, but he had to know a great deal about rotary airplane engines.

Was the residual wisdom of wheat in him but dormant? Time, temporality, practicality, and usefulness.

I have seen god die.

I was seventeen.

I had been baptized at sixteen, and, with the years, what I had accepted as truth became an instant joke when I read Nietzsche and Camus.

If god is dead, then all things are possible, including murder and adultery, but those things are possible even if god lives. Camus cautioned me, after I watched god die, that I needed a project that can be read as a reason to continue living. God is dead to me, and I see those white-haired men, in church, on their knees praying for the dead, and I think of Marcus, who says they, too, will die and their prayers mean nothing.

Religion is the non-thinker's affliction.

Wisdom, however, doesn't seem to be an infectious disease.

When god died, I felt a sense of release, a sense of relief and an absolute happiness that I was free from fear and free from *hope*—the religion-induced disease that denies the Now in favor of the Later.

As I aged, I learned that I did not need god in order to lead a moral life. I did not need religion in order to lead an ethical life. As I read more about the world, I learned how much people have struggled with freedom. It is as if freedom unleashes in us some kind of primordial fear of being. And, as I read about biology and evolution, I learned that "to be" is not a question but an imperative.

At that point I understood the need some people have for a god, but I also saw that god was not necessary if I accepted the facts of biology. If I accept that living cells evolve from non-living chemicals, I am free of hope. I do not need it. "I am" because my parents were and "they were" because their parents were, and so on, back into deep time, the time before names, the time of Forget.

It's enough to contemplate being as I am without a need to project another cause onto being. If I accept biology, then I accept time and mortality, and I understand Marcus as he writes: "What good are you if you do not do good to your fellow men who are locked into the same agony and terror of life that you are?"

No need for religious texts; just look around you. You see a man in need, it is your duty to help him. Morality and ethics are that simple—do what needs to be done. And, as Marcus writes, "if the man in need needs to kill you, you are at an end and that is that." Wisdom. Words. Deeds.

Wisdom is, maybe, what persists in others through time. My uncles do not need to know any longer when to plant or when to harvest the wheat, but they do have a memory of that knowledge.

Wisdom is temporal and its value passes in time or it ceases to be of value.

Is valuable the same thing as practical?

None of what we are, none of what we do makes any sense unless we, meaning "I," see the biological chain of being.

There were beasts on Earth who now are not. There are beasts on Earth that in time will not be. As we crawl into the inevitable oblivion of the Anthropocene, we can see our passing as the next stage. To accept that is wisdom. The next stage is that we will not be.

It is unfortunate that our forte is destruction and death, hatred and racism, instead of life and acceptance of the pitiable condition of the last of the hairless apes. If I accept my temporality, then I can accept my obsolescence and my irrelevancy, and I can accept that what I know ceases to be valued and practical in time.

These essays, for me, are a pathway to understanding mortality and accepting time as the great punisher. This is a wisdom I cannot pass on, so it is not a practical wisdom but an impractical one, because it is useless to anyone but me.

I have to accept the inevitable fading of importance, and as Marcus writes, shun the quest for fame.

I have to release myself from the need to be loved.

That is our biggest weakness—the need to be loved makes us sacrifice potential for temporary acceptance.

In the fleeting moments of my biological existence, that love-need is both a chain around my neck and an anchor.

For me, finding a release from that need is the final act or fiat of wisdom.

JANUARY 26

WISDOM AND DOUBT

I'm interested in wisdom and doubt because it occurs to me that doubt might be a necessary part of wisdom.

Doubt leaves the door ajar and that crack leaves room for change. I keep bumping up against both the permanence of wisdom and its transience. I ask the question: What do I tell my grandchildren? That can be a measure of wisdom—knowing what to teach children and how much room you leave for others to teach them.

To me, right now, the idea of a silent wisdom beyond knowledge is important. Not the facts—the sun will rise at 4:30 a.m. Low tide will be at 3:00 p.m. All that is recorded and comes from observation. But is it wisdom?

Are facts wisdom? Just what is it, this wisdom? I come back to a couple of points: Wisdom is knowing when to speak your mind, but also wisdom is knowing when to keep your silence.

Doubt feeds that corner of wisdom. Is what I know necessary? Does anyone want to know or need to know what I know? Can the world get by if I remain silent? Will anyone be hurt by my silence?

In his *Meditations*, Marcus burrows down into the question of kindness. Kindness, he writes, is what you show your fellow man because there is a social contract. Marcus writes that you should avoid fame, because fame is simply the words of mortals, and the words of mortals are transient. Memory fades, and in time, nature eats everything, and no memory resides in dead men.

What makes Marcus important to me is that he wrote *Meditations* for himself. When he writes, "it is *your* duty," he means it is his, Marcus Aurelius', duty to be kind and humble and to avoid fame or the glamour of fame, and that it is in the writing that the wisdom resides, because if it is not written, the wisdom goes silent over time.

It is the written word that appears to give wisdom its permanence. But as Marcus writes, time changes everything and tomorrow the world will be different than it is today. Nothing is permanent, and that is the dilemma of silence.

I come back to the question: "Why do I need to pass on what I know if what I know will already be antiquated by the time I can tell anyone anything about it?"

That raises the question: "What do I have that is not vanity?" Thomas Gray writes, "the boast of heraldry, the pomp of power and all that beauty, all that wealth ever gave, awaits alike the inevitable hour, the paths of glory lead but to the grave."

So, it is both vanity and ego that drive me. I want to be remembered. But wisdom of time tells me that memory dies with the man. Memory fades with time. Written or not, wisdom becomes irrelevant over time and ideas become obsolete, and there is no permanence except the permanence of my silence and my death.

There are pictures that will never go away, if I were a painter, so maybe technology changes wisdom and changes who is wise. But what if only fools and idiots survive? What, then, is wisdom?

My mother died in March. She had a quiet patience that needed no words to sanctify it. She, in her stoicism, did not burnish either her ego or her image. She had no interest in passing down what she was, but she did want to pass down what she had seen. It was important to her that others knew what she had seen.

In that, I think my mother came as close to showing her ego as she ever did. In a way, she was Marcus's ideal—selfless, kind, generous, unimposing, quiet. A stoic who did not complain, a person who did not sing her own praises.

What she knew—her wisdom—was scant. She did not give anyone advice.

Doubt and silence are big parts of wisdom—maybe it's best to remain silent—but can you show kindness through silence?

In my marriage, I have come to see two things. One: Love is cyclical. Marriage is a mechanism that lets love die, then be reborn. Two: Love is best defined for me as knowing enough not to say the one thing that will kill it. I'm cycling back here to previous thoughts—*pensées*, as Pascal called them—no coherent or far-reaching plan, just thoughts about love and doubt, about silence and love, and the ineffable feeling that comes from seeing the one you love.

Early on, I knew that love was a completeness—love at a certain point means that you, meaning *me*, want to be in the skin of the loved one, to be incorporated into the loved one, to feel her all around you—until the possession becomes so acute you can't breathe. So acute that when she is not in your eyes, you do not see, unless she is in your lungs, you do not breathe, and unless she is in you, you do not exist.

But love that intense cannot go on.

Love is cyclical. You love for a while so intensely you hurt, you dream only of the loved one, and then, as if to preserve your body and your mind, you let love pause, you let love settle, and for a long time, it is only the presence that matters, not the bodily essence inhaled. Time runs in cycles and love runs in epicycles on the rim of time. One day, you look again at the object of desire and you cannot breathe again. Your eyes are filled again and you see again with complete and total awe, and it is enough to touch, to kiss, to drive the breath away from your chest. But where is love in the body? Is it as ephemeral as Eric Kandel's quest for the Freudian ego, id, and superego in the brain?

Is love unnatural wisdom?

Marcus sets nature as the ideal; nature is everything. It is good and it is evil. It is love and death and enchantment and reason, and reason changes just as love changes through its seasons. In the heat of summer, the flower seems eternal and forever vital, but nature with its cycles admits only change. So love, too, as nature must change and go through its birth to life and death and rebirth. Is that wisdom?

Is knowing when to wait for love to be reborn wisdom?

If so, then wisdom is also patience. Marcus does not write about patience except as he understands waiting. Waiting is a part of patience, as is silence and also doubt.

Doubt leads to examination.

It is said that the unexamined life is not worth living. Without doubt, there can be no examination, only acceptance, and then you are in religion.

Without question, doubt is not plunging heedlessly into a pool of water, but first testing the depth for sharks and snakes. Doubt leads to examination, and doubt leads to the examination of love, because love is more than a feeling. *Love*. What is love?

What is the nature of love if nature is transient and love goes the way of all flesh? Love, as with wisdom, can outlive life if it is written about, but then only the words remain, never the feeling that drove the words into existence.

With words, I cannot even suggest or maybe I can only suggest the depth of love in the body and its biological imperative.

Is love wisdom or is love a biological survival trait that DNA buries in us?

As Marcus says, nature is everything and everything returns to some state of being and nothing is ever lost, just transformed. Conservation of matter. Yet love is not matter but feeling and feeling is nature and nature runs in cycles.

Marcus sees nature and all its changes, and his questions lead to deeper queries about the nature of questioning itself.

Questions, not answers, must be the true depth of wisdom.

Might wisdom be not telling another what to think or believe but telling the other, you must doubt, you must ask, you must question everything?

JANUARY 29

THE WISDOM OF DEATH

Today, I'm working some more on the question of wisdom.

How do you know you're wise?

How do you know when you're not?

Do stupid people know they are being stupid?

I want to write a little bit about the wisdom of death.

I know now of the difference between dying and death. There are stages in dying as exact and material and as physical as the stages of embryonic development. Dying starts in the brain or in the corpus. The steps are an exact process of shutting down the body and mind.

When my mother died, the process was fifteen years long. First, bits of her mind shut down. Memory was there but erratic. Then, parts of the body failed. A minor stroke paralyzed her right side. Then, the eyes—she quit reading. Years before, she had stopped driving. We used to play card games when I visited, but one day she was no longer interested in that and so we talked. But her talk consisted only of a series of questions often repeated. Where do you live? Do you have any children? Are you married? Where was I born? How many children do I have?

As the mind and memory failed, the body followed. Having always been physical—walking, working, on the go—my mother stopped cooking one day. She stopped cooking because she could not remember to turn off the skillet or to finish off the rice. And, as her body failed, she lost any interest in food. As she failed more, she lost her teeth, and as she shrank, her gums shrank too, and she could not wear dentures and so ate only soft processed foods that Gabriela fixed for her.

And then, as memory eroded more, my mother became silent. My sisters and I, my wife, and Gabriela knew it was time to take her from the house to a place where she would have long-term care.

In the care home, her body shrank more and we watched and listened to her silence. She no longer moved, except when the aide came to change her clothes or to fix up the bed.

And then, she just stopped eating.

Her only intake was water. As she dehydrated, her organs—her kidneys, her liver, her lungs—shut down, but that is not a fast process. The body—no matter how ancient, no matter how decrepit—does not let go easily of life.

So my mother shrank in size, shrank down to seventy pounds.

A human at seventy pounds is bone and skin and fingernails and toenails, all residual elements of the embryo from which it comes.

At this, the last stage, the body doesn't need nourishment or water as it shuts down. My mother, in her final stage of dying, had her private hallucinations. Momentary flashes of memory came without words, just a simple nonverbal muttering as her hands moved with involuntary gestures. As the body shuts down, the liver stops processing the bloodstream.

No urine remains in the bladder, because the kidneys are no longer processing the blood. And, the body shuts down. As the body shuts down, as the liver and kidneys and heart shut down, so, too, does the brain cease to be engaged and there are no more memories—not even the private dreams without words. And then, the eyes close.

There is no sudden resistance to dying because the body no longer lives in the world but lives in silence. There are no twitches, no dramatic final theatrical clutchings of the hand, no tears, just silence as complete as all silence of all time.

The call came at 11:00 p.m. My sister called to tell me that our mother was dead. The dying had begun years before in the eyes and in the brain and it came to an end on a soft white bedsheet at 10:45 p.m. on a Thursday in March.

The exact time, the exact place, the exact moment of the last breath is known. And then, there is nothing.

In death there is no wisdom, there is only death and then we are no more.

The body is not much when it will not eat or drink, when it will not dream or talk. There isn't much to us in death. In the dying of another, we can all see ourselves in our beginnings as if time ran backwards to a time before words, before blood, into a Deep Time of Forget.

Before pain and agony is the realization that death will come.

My mother was not afraid of death. We talked about that, talked about how to handle all the documents and who would say what in the wait of protracted and painful dying.

My mother was not a religious woman. She became a Methodist because she liked to dance and sing and the Baptists did neither. My mother did not care that we, as children, were not religious because she had seen dying on the farm when she grew up and she knew that after death there is no afterlife.

She knew that she was a being who came into being by chance and would go out the same way. Without the howling, without the shouting, without all the stupid nonsense of religion. For that, I am grateful.

Her wisdom was to know where she came from and how far into the past the chain of being ran and who the links on the chain were. She gave that wisdom to me and to my sisters—except the one who became a Mormon, for which I still cannot forgive her.

My mother was a wise woman who knew about money and men and their defects. In Mexico, she told me when I came to Cosalá to watch the mining, "I do not want a gold mine. Gold mines make men crazy. Give me a good, solid lead mine, give me a front loader and a truck to haul diesel to the dreamers. The smart woman doesn't want a gold mine, she mines the miners, she sees them dreaming and provides the fuel for their madness."

My mother was a wise woman who knew the value of land and water. Water, she told me in Delano one day, water will be the real gold here in this dry valley. Water. The same water she died without because her small, desiccated body would not take in any liquid. She knew so many things but I listened to only a few.

"Marry Helen," she told me, "she knows about fabric."

"Why do you have to use those ugly words, Jack, when you have so many beautiful ones?"

Wisdom. How did she get to be so wise?

What's the difference between wisdom and common sense? Can stupid people be wise? Do stupid people have any common sense? Is wisdom connected to intelligence? My mother wrote in a beautiful hand—the Palmer Method, they call it, with a hint of calligraphy.

"Make your writing as beautiful as your words."

And, she was a musician. She played the organ and piano. She sang, she knew so many things, and she was smart. She enjoyed being smart. She enjoyed smart people.

"John Freeman," she told me one day in Sanger, "John Freeman is a very smart man to have as a friend."

She knew, but how did she get wise?

How did she know to see John Freeman as a smart man?

How did she know that Helen was the right one for me?

How did she learn those things with no lessons?

Did she learn by experience? Is wisdom knowledge or is it intuition? Is intuition learned by small observations of plus and minus, of good and bad? Is intuition the result of an innate science of observation and being alive?

What happened to her wisdom as she lay on that soft white sheet dead, no longer thinking?

What happened to the wisdom of her mind?

It did not pass to me, so it is lost. Huge chunks of it are lost because I am not a wise man.

I have read books and I have written books, but I still cannot give my wisdom to my grandchildren with the certainty that my mother knew Helen was the woman I should marry. Had she seen a hundred Helens in a hundred cities? No. How, then, did she assess a woman such as Helen? And see who she really was?

It was not only that she knew fabric. No, it had to be more.

Something primeval and dark and piercing that came with the body out of the womb and before the womb, out of deep time.

In a sense, then, I have to think that my mother was born wise, but I was not.

FEBRUARY 2

WHEN WISDOM LIES DORMANT

Irrelevance slams into you at about the age of forty. At forty, you have spent thirty-five years gleaning truth out of experience, joy out of surprise, anger out of awareness. And then, you see that you are out of sync with the culture, out of sync with the age, out of sync with the times.

At forty, you see that everything you know, everything you thought you knew has become irrelevant. No one wants to know what you know. How do you know that you know something, anything? What is the difference between recall and physical memory?

Today my friend, Frank, asked me for Bob's phone number. I couldn't recall the number. The number is there, I know that I know what the number is, but I could not recall it. I glanced at the phone, at the keyboard, put my finger on the key, and there was Bob's number. Just like that.

The knowing was in the doing. I knew I knew it. I know that I know whole strings of numbers but I can't recall any one of them at will. Only when someone asks, what is your Social Security number? Then, it emerges.

So it is with being irrelevant to the culture, the age, the time—no one asks you, and because no one asks, your wisdom stays dormant. Still there, but not brought out. Not to be confused with advice, wisdom must lie in the past needing a stimulus to bring it into the present.

I have begun asking myself to pinpoint the time when I fell out of sync. It has to be a long time in the past. It has to be when I first started to be a writer. To be a writer, I had to do two things—look at the world and write about it.

Somewhere in there, I quit looking at the world around me and looked only at the world I was creating with the words.

This is all before the Late Awakening.

For years I lived in a hermetic world of words, thousands of words, all of them making complete sense to me even when they made no sense to anyone else. The constructed world took on the reality of time, of experience, of emotion. In that reality, there were characters with goals, characters in pain and agony, and one day, late in 2014, I felt a rupture in the seam of the world I had created. I looked out and awoke—all of a sudden.

The Late Awakening. It became clear to me that everything I knew, everything I had written was sealed in a deep resin of irrelevance, and every word I had written was obsolete, my existence redundant.

The Three Fates—irrelevant, redundant, obsolete—attacked me with a fury. "What are you doing?" Irrelevance asked. "Why are you doing it?" Redundancy asked. "What do you do with it?" Obsolescence asked.

And I could not answer them.

I saw with a clarity of the fathers before me that the chain to the past had broken, leaving my offspring alone in an abominable world where even the words people use do not connect to me anymore.

Dennis Must—novelist, playwright, story artist—tells me that he and I write the books we wanted to read as young men, but now, no one is interested in the worlds we create.

At a meeting with him at a bar in Seattle, I saw, for the first time, the truth of existence.

You become irrelevant at forty because you are a biological being brought into existence by biological beings, and just as you ignored your father's wisdom, now those around you ignore yours.

You have no wisdom after forty. After forty your ideas are obsolete, irrelevant, redundant. So, what do you tell your grandchildren?

I remember nothing of my father's wisdom because in my haste to grow away from him, nothing he said to me mattered. I did not need him, and if he had wisdom, it was obsolete and irrelevant and redundant. He could not understand who or what was happening in the world. Now, I stand like my father and his father, alone in a world that is not interested in anything I have to pass on.

Wisdom. How do you know what you know? How do you know what you don't know? Here's the conundrum—if I know a thing, it has become obsolete in the wild flowering of technology. So why would anyone want to know what I know, knowing that if they know it they will be shaped by the past?

That is the problem—how can knowing from the past be of any value to anyone in the present?

I have used a rotary phone. I have driven a stick shift Ford at ninety miles per hour without wearing a seatbelt. Now my phone will talk to me and make calls without me having to dial a number. My car talks to me. It will tell me to put on my seat-belt. My car will park itself. On the video screen, my car will show me the road as I am backing up. My car will tell me the way home.

Once I step into that car, everything I know is irrelevant. So what could I possibly want to know from my father's past? What could my grandchildren want to learn from me?

As someone once said, there's no future in the past. I would say there is no past in the future. But that notion conflicts with the nature of The Firsts.

So where does that leave me in the chain of being?

What I know will be of no use to my grandchildren. My own experience is isolated, and my joy is long past its full day. There is no future in the past as I look at my books on the shelf—a whole shelf of them. I have to ask, "who cares?"

Each cohort reinvents the wheel, but no one tells that cohort all wheels are round. All stories have been told. Only the costumes change.

Maybe the Late Awakening has to come to the seekers before they see that existence is a stream of simultaneous threads weaving together to produce an era.

The images of war are always images of the last war. Images of World War II become irrelevant in light of the horror that was Vietnam, which yields its meaning and truth to Desert Storm One that falls into irrelevance in the flood of images of Daesh slaughtering the winged bull, slashing women with swords, and Boko Haram kidnapping and raping hundreds of little girls. World War I is long lost, and images of that war that once wounded the minds of men have died in the blood of Syrian genocide.

My wisdom is built on the horror of Treblinka and Ravensbrück. It is built on the slaughter at the Somme, where one million men died and were eaten by rats. The Somme, where gas seared men's lungs. But that wisdom is obsolete, except in this: War is evil.

But no one believes it.

Men and women coming back from Iraq with their brains mushed will, in their own time, become irrelevant, their war wounds obsolete and their experience redundant in a world that does not value experience.

Is it possible that wisdom is transient? Can wisdom be learned and passed on, but only when it's useful and not politically charged? Useful. Wisdom has to be useful if it is to persist.

As I age, I step forward with caution. If someone asks me, "Why?" or "What about . . . ?" I have to ask myself, "do I want to answer?"

Wisdom is not just knowing what to say, but also knowing what *not* to say. Wisdom is not just knowing when to speak, but also knowing when to be silent. Silence is its own wisdom. When you see others reinventing the wheel, you do not say, "We already did that."

You do not. *No.* You go silent. Silence should never end with the next words being, "I think you . . . "

The "I" is no subject in chaos.

In my Late Awakening, I am loaded with ideas and experience, but wisdom is knowing enough to stay quiet.

Tranquility is the final wisdom, just one step shy of death.

When I asked him why he didn't write a book about his tunneling experiences, my father said, "I'm taking it all to the grave with me."

Perhaps my father was a wise man who understood obsolescence and irrelevance, and maybe he fell quiet in that wisdom. But, I'll never know.

This I do know: The next cohort will reinvent the wheel and it will be round. The wheel is always round. And they will look at the shiny new wheel and in full pride say, "Look at what we've done."

WISDOM IN DEEP TIME

Today I'm writing about the wisdom of loneliness and a sense of loss in deep time. Deep Time—that place where you have lost the links and find yourself alone. Deep Time means that where you came from is lost. In the past there is no past, only its present. There is no past in the present but only a *then* as there is only a *now* in the present.

Deep Time—no measurement of minutes, days, hours, even years, but the measure of the bodies that came, then died and are no more. In that time, as you stand on the cusp of *then*, you look back at the dreamscape and see the broken chain. For some of us, it is two generations; for others, only a short while between birth and abandonment. Abandoned, we are alone and have to discover the wisdom of loneliness for ourselves. The time of "without being." The time of *un-being*. The lost one in a time of loss and loneliness, the genetic loneliness when you lose in time all those who made you who you are and how you are.

That loneliness as you look out on Deep Time where, somewhere, you once were, but now are not, and for all of us it was a time of nakedness, then of animal skins, long before cloth.

Generational loneliness and Deep Time. You are a pivot. The one before you was a pivot—extinction just one misstep away. That loneliness of Deep Time with its lost caring and the lost beings buried now in deeper time.

Deep Time is the unbinding you feel looking out over the vastness, the empty past now devoid of the generatrix. But the wisdom of loneliness is more than a nostalgia of time and space; it is a feeling of the links in the broken chain that led to you. The wisdom of loneliness is learning how to live with mortality, how to live with the *now*, knowing that for you, the *then* can never be.

Deep Time is not a measure of days, hours, years, even centuries. Time itself is the ticking of no clock besides the beat of the element that measures eternity.

The loneliness, say, of stars in a galaxy without memory, without feeling, without knowing anything, but doing what has to be done to find their place and time.

In the late night, I sleep, but I have no memory of sleeping. I have no feeling of being. I am not, when I sleep. In sleep, there are no moments of clarity, but as I wake, first there is consciousness, then the memory of who I am, what I am, and where I am. Who am I at that moment of awakening? Am I, at that moment, all I will be, all I have been? Where does memory go when I sleep? In sleep, I am not conscious of memory, nor am I aware of sleep. I am *not* in sleep. But as I wake, consciousness is there—was it always there? And, conscious, I have a thought, a question, an image that emerges from sleep. The image from *The Seventh Seal*, of death at the seashore playing chess with a knight.

I see the image, but I cannot, as I rise to first consciousness, recall the name of the film director who made *The Seventh Seal*.

The memory of death endures, and as my mind engages with the image, a name finally emerges.

Bergman. But his first name? *No-name* Bergman. *Wild Strawberries* Bergman, *Fanny and Alexander* Bergman, *Through a Glass Darkly*—where is his name?

And then, it emerges from a somewhere past, a hidden darkness, and it is Ingmar.

Ingmar Bergman.

And now the image and the image-maker fuse and the memory is there. It was there. It did not die, but it was lost, as lost as I am in time unknown to those who came before me, not yet a memory for those who will come after me. It is that loneliness that injures me. The loneliness of dying memory, a past that once was but is not now. And in the image there is Death and the Knight. And the Knight has a face, but he has no name. He is the Knight, and I want to know his name. I need to know his name. The image of his face rolls across my mind and I see him, the Knight, transformed into an assassin years later in another image, but still his name eludes me as must the names of all those who came before names became us. It is lost, his name—it is there, in the lonely time of not being—but I cannot recall another face, this one would have a name—Max what? Can half a name die in memory, leaving only half a man? There it is. Max von Sydow. My mind has brought the Knight out of the past and into another present. I connect the names, and at last it emerges—but who is Buñuel? And who is Fellini? And where are their names in my mind and my past that now melds into my present with legs amputated, fingers severed—half man, half memory. And then, one by one, they come together—Luis Buñuel, Federico Fellini, Ingmar Bergman, Max von Sydow—and memory is complete and the past lives in the now.

When there is no edge to time there is a great loneliness and the wisdom lies in learning how to live with fragments of being alive, intact but not whole.

That is the wisdom of loneliness and its sense of loss in Deep Time.

As I read *The Brain's Architecture*, I learned that mind is what brain does. Brain runs twenty-four seven. It never rests. Pieces of it die, and with their death, the gaps in memory grow and time recedes until there is no *then*, there is no future, there is only a *now* that throbs in deepest time as memory releases its hold on you and you look out on the vast emptiness and it is there, the last residue forever forgotten.

As I read Marcus Aurelius, I see the words of a man who did not speak to me. His words are to himself. His "you" means Marcus, and he becomes a character in my past, as do all the characters in all the books I read. I am trapped in time and desperation as I look for wisdom.

In *Trio*, I wrote Jim Garret's story about sitting in his tower waiting for wisdom that never comes. Wisdom is not an active participant in my life, but a kind of passive uneasiness at the back of my mind as I, too, wait for wisdom. But I have to go into a space that scares me—that Deep Time of Forget—to learn that not everything I have known will be with me to the end. Ingmar Bergman hiding in my past: his images are fresh and real in my mind as they were the first time they entered my darkness. In the wisdom of loneliness I understand being alone, and what it means in the early morning when I become conscious again and feel the heat of Helen's body. She is still lost in sleep, unaware that she is sleeping, unaware that I feel her heat. And I ask myself—what has she lost in the loneliness of Deep Time?

Frank told me that Mary is losing pieces of him. Pieces of who he was are not with her now, and I imagine her memory as a mirror lacking big chunks of its silvering—so the reflection of the man is not complete in her eyes. That leads to her memory. Pieces of her have disappeared. She is not what or who she once was. Does she understand that the wonder is learning how to live with loss, piece by piece, until there is no memory, until she is no more?

The dead have no memory but leave only bones for a while until the bones, too, dissolve.

Marcus Aurelius writes, nature reclaims everything. Do memories exist in the dust with their bones in a skull with no brain, a brain with no mind? Are memories eternal and intact in another domain we cannot imagine, memories for processes and ideas waiting to be rediscovered?

Do birds feel the deep loneliness of Deep Time? Without writing, without history, without a sociology of birds, do birds know where they came from? And why?

My wife says, "No. They don't know what they do, they do it."

We are the only species infected with the fear of time and the loss of the past. Without a past, what are we? Without our history, are we even here? We are not as wise as birds because we have to ask the questions: "Where have we come from? Where are we going?"

We are the only species that cannot just *be*.

FEBRUARY 9

THE WISDOM OF PROGENY

Today, I write about the wisdom of children. The wisdom of grandchildren.

I've been writing about wisdom and what it is and how you get it and how you know if you don't have it. I've been writing about the creeping irrelevance of temporal wisdom and how the wisdom of one generation fades into useless knowledge and how the knowledge I have acquired becomes obsolete.

My first course in graduate school was on the use of the library system. Three days in the stacks learning all the codes and where certain categories of stored wisdom were kept on the shelves and how in the special collections library were kept all the scurrilous, exotic, erotic books—from Rétif de la Bretonne to the Marquis—and how the books of and about the Bible were catalogued under the letter designation "BS."

Now, there are no card catalogs in libraries. Everything I learned, everything I knew about libraries is passé. Not long ago, I visited Suzzallo Library at the University of Washington. There is no card catalog, but there is a computer. I typed in books about sex ratios and came up with a book titled "Too

Many Women." I was researching texts for *Citadel*, and I needed material that would have taken days, perhaps weeks, to uncover using the old system.

Too Many Women is an in-depth study of sex ratios and the cultural dynamics of sex ratios. By sex ratios, the authors mean the number of males plotted against the number of females.

There were other books on the subject, but *Too Many Women* gave me what I needed. It was only later, as I was reading the book, that I understood what had happened. The old style of research took time. The new style was measured in milliseconds. The search that would have led me to the stacks and code numbers and categories yielded a list, and from the list, I would have bought two books. No books borrowed, nothing to take back. But there were books scanned and stored that had never been checked out. Everything I knew was obsolete. Irrelevant. Redundant.

I began to wonder how much of what I know is in fact temporally redundant.

Is everything I learned of no use to anyone now living?

This is a burden I've been carrying for ten years. It brings me back to the wisdom of children and the wisdom of my grandchildren.

Is there anything I can teach them, tell them, leave with them that isn't already dead? I gave them a computer, not a ready-made, plug-and-play computer but a Kano computer kit. They had to build it from a set of parts. They put it together in an hour, and in an hour were already coding. They learned in one hour the entire object-oriented coding system they needed to construct images on the screen, to build their own games, and to make new things they had never seen before.

I recall my first meeting with the computer. It was a naked box with two floppy drives. I needed something to run on it. I went to the computer center at the university, where I was told about freeware I could download. I handed the tech a floppy disk.

He said, "do it yourself."

"I don't know how," I told him.

He took me to a desk, inserted my floppy into a drive and the disk with the program I wanted into another drive and he typed "copy a:b." And—there was my program.

I knew nothing. But I watched my grandchildren construct the computer from scratch. They already knew what I had spent years acquiring, getting me to the question of a built-in epigenetic wisdom that isn't learned but comes with the times.

In time, I asked myself what else they knew as if by cultural osmosis. It turned out they already knew about coding and books, and they were able to design and write and print books that had nothing to do with the kind of story I would have them write. It came to me that if I persisted in trying to "teach" them what I knew, I would in fact impede their progress and development. What can a grandfather give his grandchildren?

It puzzled me for a while, and then a few years ago, I realized I could teach them about money.

No matter what age, what time, what culture, a person has to know about money in a modern civilization and has to know methods of transition. So, I gave them money.

In small increments. I told them the value of money and why they needed to know its value. I taught them how to balance their bank accounts, and I taught them about debit and credit. I got them working a cash register, and for a while, I felt useful, I felt important. I had taught my grandchildren about money.

Then, one day, Alex told his grandmother, "I need a credit card, Grandma."

"Why do you need a credit card, Alex?"

"Amazon needs my credit card number, Grandma."

Alexander had gone online using his hand-built computer and had found books and games he wanted on Amazon, but Amazon needed his credit card number. Right away, I saw that my money system had holes in it. My entire approach to cash was obsolete. No one carries cash because you can't use cash in an electronic universe.

My grandchildren are wiser about their times than I am. I look at the writing table at Louisa's coffee shop. I pay with a five-dollar bill for the cup of coffee while my other friends use credit cards. I am a dinosaur in the company of electronic beings. Most of what I know works the same way, bringing me to the notion of the simultaneity of ideas.

Nothing ever really dies. In some factory, in some city, somewhere, they still manufacture candle snuffers. Now, however, there are electric candles that do not need snuffing.

Candle snuffers—obsolete, but still there.

I pull into a gas station in my car. As I pull in, I see a Tesla pass by. Electric. Gas. Simultaneous threads in a complex culture.

Obsolete, but still there.

Helen and I have taken a new tack in entertainment. We now allot five hours a week to New.

We search the TV for new programs, new ideas, and we record them. We watch the new shows.

"What did they say?" I ask my wife.

"I don't know," she says.

We sit in total ignorance of what's happening in front of us and then go to a show for Old People. Shows in which there are no actors under the age of forty.

We see them locked in their own temporal wisdom. No one under the age of thirty can understand them. Audrey who? Marilyn what?

And then we read.

Every night we read for an hour or so—all old stuff. Stuff printed years ago. Stuff that means nothing to anyone under the age of twenty. *Too Many Women*. Cultural constructs resulting from skewed sex ratios. I see what's happening in the culture, but the people it's happening to have no idea what is happening to them. The ideas in my head? Where are they? Can they be replaced with new ideas the way I can now change the names of the characters in *Citadel* by using the search-and-replace function?

When I wrote my first novel, I used carbon paper to make copies. If I needed to change a character's name, I could not do it without retyping the entire manuscript. There was a manuscript to change then. There is no manuscript now. Electronic submissions only. When I sent *Trio* to my publisher, I emailed a PDF.

When she sent back her edits, they were in a "text editor" with changes in little boxes along the sides in the margins. Accept all changes? *Sure, why the fuck not?*

How much of what I know now about writing a novel is of any use to any other human being?

At one writing session, fellow writer Laura Nelson asked what I thought she should write about. I hesitated. My brain sped over all the pitfalls and traps of that question, and as I gave her an idea, I was punished by my stupidity. How could anything I knew be of use to another human being when what I knew about money was of absolutely no use to my grandchildren?

Telling Laura anything about writing is like teaching my grandchildren to use a hand crank auger to bore holes in wood. The wisdom of an age dies with the owner. Every generation has its own wheel to reinvent. Its own mousetrap. But now the inventions are genetic snippers that allow a scientist to rewrite the entire genetic code of a species. In that, I am lost.

FEBRUARY 12

THE WISDOM OF SILENCE

Up to the age of twenty-two, I acted solely on a desire to destroy human dignity and to disrupt, without knowing what I was doing—morality, ethics. These actions enhanced my innate misanthropic tendency.

I had learned very little beyond the "*fornicative* arts," and the ability to prevaricate. In short—I did not know what wisdom was.

In time, I met men and women who taught me about ethics, taught me that morality is not an extension of my dick, and that misanthropy is a juvenile position to hold. I did not understand two things—evolution is an irreversible mistake resulting in the universal state of human unhappiness, and given that, the horrible place of human beings on the constantly evolving Earth is to be a source of pity, not condemnation. Most of the stupidity resulted from not understanding the value of poetry.

Later, I wrote that I did not have the wisdom of birds or the patience of flowers.

And then, I met the woman I married. She taught me everything I needed to know, but still, and even then, I did not know what to do with what I had learned. Wisdom, I thought, is knowing what to do, knowing when to do it, and, as I learned through many bad episodes—wisdom is knowing what not to say, what not to do.

Wisdom has something to do not just with experience, with knowledge and age, but silence.

In an intermediate phase in my becoming, I met many screenwriters who told me that the perfect movie is a near-silent one. Not 1920-silent, but a silent screen where action and image dominate. Stories, the screenwriters tell us, are told through action and image. Many novelists do not understand this even though we live in an age of images, an age of action. Thought takes a backseat to action. The screenwriters say that you can't film a thought, you can film only behavior—what the actor does. But what is not said may in time be seen as what is best. Silence.

As I age, I understand more the value of silence. The reasons are simple—most of what I know is irrelevant to the age I am in, all of what I know has become obsolete to that age, and everything I could possibly say is redundant. It has all been said before. Everything we, in our brightness, do is an extension of The Firsts.

Wisdom is knowing enough not to repeat what is already known and by being known has become clichéd and ugly. Ugliness is a great concern for me, now. I think I was at my best when I moved like liquid over smooth stone, in absolute silence. There is something tranquil about the body in motion without sound that becomes sublime. It needs no language to explain it. It is like talking about music. Music is best done, not talked about, and so it is with being—best done and not talked about, best done in silence.

In the past, I listened to music while I worked. Sometime in the last ten years, I stopped the music but I did not stop the rhythm. Now, I work in total silence and the silence has a measure of peace to it, a separation from the fury of being. I asked John Verrall, a composer, pianist, philosopher, what he considered the ideal a man should reach for. He told me it was mastering the art of sitting in silence.

When I became deaf, I did not know I was deaf. I had descended into a silent world that was not of my choosing. I withdrew, as deaf people sometimes do. But then, at my wife's insistence, I got hearing aids. I realized that the choice was mine—silence or noise or non-silence. As of late, I am choosing silence.

In the morning, I do not put in my hearing aids but work, eat, walk, and exercise in silence. When I lift weights, all I feel is my lungs working, my body tensing and relaxing. I do not hear the breath leave and enter my body. I float in a world of silence, although from time to time, I do hear the steel weights hit the floor or clang together as I lift, and that interruption startles me. Broken silence.

Wisdom is, for me, silence, age, experience, knowledge. But can I teach my grandchildren to adore silence? Why should I? Let them experience noise, music, voices, the sounds of birds chirping. My wisdom is not transferable to the next generation because my knowledge and experience are temporal relics—the books I have read are always the books I now write or want to write. I am, as my friend Dennis Must, tells me—a Gutenbergian. "Gutenbergian" means that what I write is, the instant I write it, already archaic. Temporal wisdom is mere practice. Wisdom is a web of being in time, melded with experience and knowledge. But as I've written before, what I know now is of no use to anyone and it seems that some aspect of wisdom has to be usefulness.

Were I a priest in Babylon, I would know the orbit of Venus, and knowing that orbit, I would know when to tell the farmers to plant their seed. Knowing the orbit of Venus to a farmer is useful because he has to plant at the right time in the right season. If he does not, his seed will rot. It will decay or it will burn and he will lose the crop and he will starve and his fledglings will starve. He will vanish from the Naturally Wise world that did not need him. That does not need any of us.

Wisdom in another time was useful. It had meaning in real time and to real people. But now wisdom is transitory. Transient.

I read the *Meditations* of Marcus Aurelius. He is a wise man—he talks to "you," but he means "me, Marcus." What he tells himself is that life is transient, it is temporary, while rebirth and nature are everything and everything comes from silence and returns to nature, even the songs of birds. Life returns to decay, and from decay, life comes new. The natural wisdom I disparaged at twenty-two now lives in its purity beyond anything we know or can know or have ever known.

How does this wisdom, over two thousand years old, work for me in my silence? I don't know. But I have to ask myself, "is silence surrender?"

It is for me a deep question that comes from the nature of knowledge. Why learn anything if it only rots? Why teach anyone anything if they die and return to nature? Is there a species of nihilism in wisdom?

Deep in Marcus—I now call him Marcus as I've grown to know him—there is this bit of wisdom: All that matters to the man is the social bond. Men and women bonded to one another to do one thing: pass on the bond and live in their pity and hopelessness divorced from the cycles and epicycles of an existence that has no meaning and will reveal none. We hold one another, in one way or another, and we sing our helplessness as a multiplicity bonded in a delusion of meaning derived from our own stupidity.

The goal of wisdom could be to pass on the *now*, not the temporal *now* but the *eternal now* that is civilization. Oh, Civilization. It is all we have. Birds know nothing of civilization and flowers have no need of cities.

Can I call myself civilized if I live in silence, gaining knowledge and experience as I age but deciding not to pass on what I know?

The wheel.

Most of what I know is of no use, yet could, perhaps, be useful but for this inconvenient truth: No one chooses in this time of ascending ignorance to learn the wisdom of the elders because the elder in his silence is irrelevant. In the Age of COVID-19, the elderly are disposable. Disposable absorbers of resources and goods best used to preserve the young. Yet, the moral reality of a civilization is the way it treats the elderly. In America, in the twenty-first century, the elderly with their temporal, fading, useless wisdom are disposable. America has retrieved the Spartan ideal and is leaving the elderly on the hillside, in the heat, in the cold—to die. Marcus. Marcus.

"What possible use can I have for wisdom that is seventy-five years old?" the young ones say.

I reply, "But we did that already and it didn't work."

The wheel.

Every generation has to reinvent the wheel. What no generation knows beforehand is that their wheel will only be as round as the wheel of the previous generation. When D.H. asked me to help him become a poet, I told him, "This is not a conversation. I talk, you listen."

Years into the poetics, he still has not finished reinventing his wheel. My knowledge, my experience, my age, my wisdom are of no use to him. My wisdom decays in disuse with no poetic progeny. But what has been lost?

What, then, do I teach my grandchildren? Will they listen to me? Probably not, and with reasons of their own. They have a time and place where what I know cannot help and might hurt them: "No, Grandpa, we don't do it like that now."

"No, Grandpa, that's the old way."

I once read a book in which the author had written, "To learn new things, read old books."

Wisdom is crippled by the speed of knowledge in our age. What was new a year ago, yesterday, is old—of no use. Look at this: I read an article about scientists who had found that two different genes could take the place of the Y chromosome, a gamete, and from that gamete produce living offspring. Just last year, science told me the Y chromosome was absolutely necessary for the production of offspring. But now, this knowledge that at one time was wisdom is passé. Knowledge is moving too fast, now. We are the instruments of our own destruction.

I cannot tell if what I know will remain in time, but this I do know: silence heals.

What is not said is deeper than all words. Wisdom is transient. Knowledge returns to dust. The only thing that remains is experience, and that for only as long as the fleshy shell survives. Marcus writes that the bond is the sole purpose. The biologist writes that offspring are the sole purpose. The geneticist writes that duplication of DNA is the sole purpose.

In two thousand years, all we have done is verify Marcus' notion, because in the end, it is the bond that ensures the future for this despondent, useless, overly productive hairless ape whose *fornicative* excesses slaughter the birds and uproot the flowers, leaving a sea of plastic that will endure thousands of years.

What is human wisdom but a temporal, transient understanding of process, excess, product, and progeny? Where is the beauty and ecstasy of sex if the bond is replication, product, process?

In my novel, *Citadel,* the protagonist Daiva writes about being human. She asks, is a *parthenogyne* human if she is born via processes besides XY gamete fertilization, meiosis, and mitosis?

I do not know the answer to that question. Yet.

FEBRUARY 16

IS KNOWLEDGE WISDOM?

I keep coming back to this series of rhetorical questions because I am not sure what wisdom is.

What is it?
How do you get it?
How do you know you have it?
Do you ever know that you don't have it?
Is there a stupid wisdom?

I think wisdom has something to do with knowledge through time. That's the temporal side of wisdom. But wisdom wears out. A man whose wisdom has worn out finds that he is irrelevant. Waiting to die. He's obsolete, his wisdom has passed into nothingness. He is redundant. A body among billions of bodies doing nothing. Waiting to die while inventing fantasies about divinity and eternal life.

When I was young, I read books. I learned several languages. I studied literature and history. I studied mythology and linguistics. I studied in close-reading the work of C.S. Peirce, the mythologies of Claude Lévi-Strauss, and I studied—with repeated readings—the work of C.G. Jung.

I studied biology and evolutionary genetics, I studied social dynamics and game theory, but as I sit here, today, writing this, I ask myself, "where is the wisdom in all that? Is there even one thing, one idea I can pass on to others that is not simply a rephrasing of an idea I learned from my reading?" Wisdom has a little to do with knowledge but not a lot to do with how to use it. Wisdom is a way to extend the reach of The Firsts without losing your fingers.

My friend, mystery writer Robert Ray, thinks that wisdom is what minds in time reduce to aphorisms.

The aphorism and the witticism come if the writer—like Aesop or de La Rochefoucauld, Confucius, or Jean de La Fontaine—reduces experience and knowledge to a simple saying that has thousands of years of time behind it. In a sense, the total wisdom of being can be found either in *The Analects of Confucius* or *The Art of War* by Sun Tzu. The former takes his wisdom from four thousand years of Chinese experience and breaks it out in modes of behavior of a social nature, while Sun Tzu uses that same experience to direct the mind through conflict. The Bible is useless as wisdom when compared to *The Analects* and *The Art of War*. Peace and conflict are the poles of the duality. This relates to Lévi-Strauss and the polarities of myth, which become nodes to explain existence. Each polarity has to be resolved, and its resolution comes to rest in the domain of a second set of polarities—raw and cooked. The poles are mediated by an action that produces the change from raw to cooked, from conflict to peace. No word has meaning away from other words. This is the basic fact of language and dictionaries. To define a word requires the existence of other words, each standing in the stream where each word has equal potential until set in its semantic context. Homophones are a good example of this. Seam/seem, until written, are the *same* sound that is an anagram of *seam*—the spoken is necessarily ambiguous until set against a cosmos of other words, each of which is part of a triad—icon, index, symbol.

In this, C.S. Peirce enters the world of Confucius and Sun Tzu and Lévi-Strauss, where semantics are systems and need a lexicon. The lexicon is the river of words. Seam and seem are free until locked together in some sort of sign system—and out of this complex, with enough time, there is born something akin to knowledge. And yet, wisdom does not proceed directly from agglutinated facts.

It always comes back to the same question: Where is knowledge? Is it just the lexicon? The dictionary? Knowing flows from the words put together to index meaning. Words are either at the root of wisdom or they give way to the gesture—doing. In this specific ordering of words, we get close to art.

Saying—doing.

A kind of Lévi-Straussian polarity. The wisdom of the saying is this—do not tell, show. The deep artist goes beyond showing to evoking. It is better to show than to tell; it is better to evoke than to show. In evoking, mind connects to mind. The Bond that Marcus worships. Human to human bound up in our useless, helpless egosphere in which each of us is the sole occupant of any importance.

All this depends on the lexicon and where it resides in the mind. Mind, as neuroscientists tell us, is what the brain does. A man learns from books and from doing—saying and doing. But let us say he has a bike accident and goes into a coma. Is he still a wise man if he can't retrieve his wisdom?

If we sleep, where does our wisdom go? It is in the retrieving in time of knowledge and experience that knowledge and experience meld into wisdom. Wisdom is more than facts.

Is what is not said wisdom, or is it only in the saying that wisdom emerges? I know that love floats in time in great cycles. Marriage is a way to bond while love floats away, leaving enough time for it to return.

The one time when love does not return is the one time the lover says the one thing that should not be said. The relationship is always fragile and in its fragility can be shattered and once shattered can never be brought back.

So where does love live? In the mind? In the body? In the brain? Is love wisdom? Is wisdom love? When the lover says the one thing that should not be said, is the lover being wise?

Wisdom and silence.

Wisdom and the saying.

Two sides of the polarity of life.

Action and silence.

As I age, I grow. As I grow, I assess. As I assess, I learn the temporality of wisdom, and what I know passes from my *now* into the cultural past. At that moment, I become irrelevant.

The question then is this: Does everything I know become obsolete at this same moment?

From *The Analects*, I learned that silence is golden—that which is not said expresses the wisdom of the negative. That which is said and tears apart the relationship cannot be wisdom.

But is wisdom a cultural endowment that all members of society will share or is wisdom an artifact of the ego?

I don't know.

In my poem, "Beckett's Boils," Beckett answers all questions in one voice—"I do not know."

Can a person enter into society and still remain silent?

Marin Marais taught us that *le petit badinage* is the cultural grease that keeps society moving. The silent man seems to have nothing to offer and so appears to be dumb because it is only in the saying and then in the writing that the unknown becomes known.

Can a problem be solved in silence without words or writing, without numbers or equations?

I do not know.

All my wisdom then can be reduced to a single phrase—I do not know.

The answer to any question.

All I know is the residual evolutionary response to a cultural stimulus.

In *Citadel*, Trisha tells Rose, "I go to the beach to find a man. I find a man because I want to have sex. I want to have sex because I want to have a baby. I want to have a baby, because I am a woman and women have babies. And without a baby, I am not a woman. I am nothing but a string of residual evolutionary responses strung together in a false and fake stream of living that is supposed to make me human. And I am sick of being automatic, Rose. I am automatic. I am human. I think I choose but there is another deepness making the choice—the residue of evolution in me—and I want it to end. But there is nothing to replace it. Bound to the past, my gonads dictate what I will do. Even when I take the pill, I cannot stop, because not to have a baby doesn't mean evolution stops being in control. I want out, Rose, but I do not want to die yet."

As I read Marcus Aurelius' *Meditations* I asked myself—does his wisdom span two thousand years with more reach than a religious text?

What Marcus writes is his personal wisdom cast out into a universal voice that is directed at the You, but the You is always the writer himself.

The You is always and forever only the writer himself.

At the same time, I am reading a book called *Life's Engines: How Microbes Made Earth Habitable*.

Will my search for wisdom ever end?

FEBRUARY 19

THE WISDOM OF THE DEAD

Is wisdom temporal and eternal or simply carnal? Does the temporal wisdom of a person become irrelevant the moment carnality vanishes?

Today, I write about the wisdom of the dead. When I was young, I, like every teenage boy, believed I was immortal. I believed that nothing bad could ever happen to me. I believed I would live forever and forever be young. But my first insight into death came one day when Bill Hansen and I were on our way back to Sanger from Fresno. Bill was driving crazy, humping his Merc up to ninety miles per hour on Highway 180, Kings Canyon Highway up to Del Ray Avenue, where a car entered the roadway after making a rolling California stop. Bill braked—hard—and the Merc slewed around, tail end pointed east. Bill brought the car to a stop, passenger side inches from the gas pump of the Texaco station at the corner of Del Ray and 180.

We sat there—the engine still idling—knowing we were close to death that day. We knew it, but nothing changed our behavior.

Bill popped the Merc into first and we headed to Sanger at eighty miles per hour. That, as I recall, was my first scent of death.

Later, I learned that there is a big gap between death and dying.

Death can come all at once, or it can sneak up on you. But there is only one state in death—dead.

Dying is another world altogether.

Dying can be slow, dying can take time, there are phases to dying. There are plateaus to dying, there are stages of the body shutting down, the brain closing off, the loss of mind, the fecal reality of the dying sphincter, and the uremic reality of the dying bladder.

At that time, the body no longer needs food or drink, and this shows when you cannot swallow. You are dying.

I saw this first when my older sister Nancy was dying of kidney cancer. My sister J and I took her to the UCLA Medical Center for exploratory surgery after her diagnosis.

At UCLA, the surgeon made his incisions, and right off, sewed her back up. “It is too late,” he told us. “The cancer has metastasized to both kidneys, her lungs, and her liver.”

We took Nancy back to Bakersfield to die. Dying was a three-month process.

I called her every day, and as soon as I heard her voice, I knew the stage, the phase of her dying. At first, her usual jolly, sisterly voice was still there, and then, as the phases progressed, the voice turned faint and weak. It was then that I went to her. My sister J and I shared our sister’s dying.

We watched her fall into that forever dark place of the forever closed eyes. We watched her as she wove the air with her hands as if pulling on imaginary gloves. We did not know what she was seeing. Perhaps setting silverware on the table? We did not know. As she lay dying, she was living a dream of dreams, but we did not know what it was. There is that about death. That unknown space between words.

And then came the absolute silence, the unmoving hands, the unblinking eyes, the absence of REM. The dream had stopped. My sister was dead.

We stood in the odor of death.

As your sister dies, there is one last act. It is not the death rattle or the long sigh of death. It is not that shuddered breath that Jack Moodey wrote about. No. The final act of dying is the evacuation of the bowel. There is no more terrible finality—because in dying, Nancy gave back the earliest of her controls.

For fifty-six years, she had control of her body, of her bladder, of her anal sphincter, but in dying it was no longer hers.

I can now write about her dying without tears. Tears. My own body reacting to her death.

I can now remember her voice in all its fullness without that deep agony of knowing that she is dead.

A sister dies in pieces. I had no sense that day Bill Hansen and I shook the hand of death that there was more to death. The dying.

Later, I learned of the agony of waiting to die when I received a letter from my friend, Deborah Russell. I wrote her story in a novel titled, *A German Romance*. She was a scion of the Dudeks of Poland. She had an ancestor who had slept with Napoleon. She was a proud woman, full of vigor and love and ripe in her sexuality. In her letter, she told me how much she loved me and how much she would miss me. After reading those words, I called her but she did not answer.

I called a friend who knew the man Deborah was living with. "She is dead," he told me. And there is that silence of the dead still living in the minds of the lovers.

Deborah had been in agony. Not the agony of cancer, or the fear of death, but her mind lived in her horrific past, a past where she had found her mother sprawled drunk on the stairs to their third-floor apartment—Deborah was six. Life did not get better for her. In her thirty-second year, she swallowed a full prescription of phenobarbital. Thirty tablets. She pulled on a heavy overcoat, filled her pockets with rocks, and walked into Lake Berryessa.

She did not know this was a copy of Virginia Woolf's final act.

I miss her, Deborah Russell, scion of a Polish princess who had sex with Napoleon.

Later, death and dying came back to me. First, my father, who in his muddled and angry mind died when he fell onto a rock in the garden. His death was not a trauma to me or to my sisters, because he was not a gentle man, nor was he a good father. But he was a man.

His dying was not in the agony of slow dying, but a quick hour to death. I was not there. But I knew the end. It is always the same, the same smells. The final act is the same. The body that held itself unsullied for eighty-four years releases its effluvia—and all men, all women, are, in the final act, the same, just as their blood is the same and their tears are the salt of pain, the same, as are all their lost connections in Deep Time.

And then, the wisdom of the dead speaks. In the final moment of agony, there is no light, there is no vision, there is no soul to wander with Dante in purgatory, for there is no purgatory, there is no soul except in the mind of the living.

In the mind of the dying, there must be a clarity to let itself be seen.

My mother lay dying in the natural sequence of dying—on a bed with clean sheets, in a room with clean air, in a city where her family, what remained of it, watched her.

As she lay dying, she opened her eyes. "Am I dying?" she asked.

"No, Verda, you are not dying."

"Yes I am. I'm dying for some chocolate."

And in that night, in the quiet and empty night, dying, she stopped eating. She stopped drinking. She reacted as did all her ancestors lost in Deep Time whom she could never know but whose blood she shared. We know that. The blood carries on through time, the blood of the dead circulates through the heart of the living.

In dying we are tropisms that react to light, to touch, react to heat and smell, but dead, there is no feeling, no sense of agony. No wisdom.

Dead, my mother was exactly as dead as my sister, my father, exactly as dead as Ruby von Dudek, as dead as her mother, her father, her brothers, her sisters.

Death makes no bets and plays no favorites.

This I learned from reading the *Meditations* of Marcus Aurelius: In the end, no matter how well or how poorly you live, your death takes you back to nature and from nature there is no return.

I know that my mother was not a religious woman.

She would have liked the materialist philosophy of Marcus Aurelius because she knew that, after the end, there is nothing. All religion is bullshit.

This also I learned from Marcus: It is the community of being that is a measure of all things, and the explanation for being is the community. Live and then die, and all who praise you will die and in the darkness of death there is the final voicing: in that all humans, all animals are equal, we share the same fate.

In the final moment, we all loosen the anal sphincter, no matter what we know, what we have done, where we have been. Our final act is the odor of our death.

FEBRUARY 23

THE WISDOM OF MARRIAGE

Today, I'm writing about the wisdom of marriage.

Marriage.

To know the word is to peer into the deepest cave of human behavior. There is a biological presence in marriage. Out of the two come one—half and half—and in the haploid reality there is the impulse to couple—to join together.

In *Citadel*, there is one question: What is a human?

Lynn Margulis and co-author Dorion Sagan write in *Acquiring Genomes* that sex is the exchange of genes. Bacteria, they write, exchange genes from moment to moment in parallel. Bacteria have adapted so fast we can't keep up with them.

Humans can exchange genes once every nine months. As species go, we are slackers. Marriage does not occur in bacteria, does not occur in most species, although as the ethologists and biologists write—some species mate for a lifetime.

In humans, marriage has not just a biological imperative, but a social one. Marriage is what you do unless you don't want to marry. Not wanting to do it is a recent phenomenon.

Why do men focus on quantity—how many times a month, a week, a day, they have sex? How many children a man produces is a measure of his fertility and worth. But it is not the men who bear the children. The women bear the children. In earlier sociobiological thinking, there was a saying—sperm are cheap, eggs are expensive.

In every ejaculation, the average male spews three hundred million sperm into the world. Most women produce, at most, two ova a month. So, in the cheapness of sperm, there is a sociology of sex. Men are careless, women are careful. Marriage can be seen as a mechanism to ensure a presence in a dyad that at one time needed that presence.

In *Too Many Women*, a book about sex ratios—males to females—the authors write about a process for signaling the behavior of humans. In cultures where there are more men than women, women are treasured and sometimes kept isolated. In this, there is a deep biology—the biology of paternity. Sociobiologists explain the stepparent in such clear terms it is amazing we have not seen it before—the stepparent will only with great reluctance invest resources in another's offspring.

There is a timeless selfishness in the genes.

"That kid ain't mine," the stepparent says.

Sarah Hrdy wrote about the langur monkeys. In her work, she reports that when the alpha male is displaced in a troop, the new alpha kills the offspring of the old alpha, sending the females in the troop into estrus to mate with the new alpha. These males do not want to share paternity. Sperm is cheap—all males of the mammalian species have too many sperm, yet the biology to explain that is still in the making. It relates in some way to size.

The ova of all species are huge in comparison to the size of the Y chromosome. Of the three hundred million sperm, one, perhaps two, rarely three make it through the wall of the ovum. Eggs are not only expensive, they are very selective.

Selectivity is at the root of marriage and selectivity is at the root of natural law—rape is a violation not just of the female's body but a violation of the entire process of sexual selection in evolution. The females of all species choose the males with the best genes. Genes are best shown in resources, behavior, and beauty. In *The Rape of Troy*, Jonathan Gottschall cites Irven DeVore—males are a breeding experiment run by women. In *The Rape of Troy*, an application of evolutionary biology to *The Iliad* and *The Odyssey*, Gottschall writes that Greek women chose the strongest, most beauteous, most resourceful males, while Greek males made themselves strong, beautiful, and resourceful so that women would choose them. It was a cycle of fitness. Marriage was a reward—to the handsomest, strongest, most invested male went the hand of the woman, and in marriage, she made a pact to receive his Y chromosome and to rear his young.

Marriage can be seen as the climax of the breeding experiment run by women. We live in a unique time. I call it the Niche. In *Citadel*, I write about Western women who can be educated, own property, work, own a business, and choose their sexual partners without the usual cause and effect—sex equals child. Child equals home. Home equals solitary living, isolation, desperation.

Western women have taken control of their ova. Women in the West set the tone. Women in the West can display their bodies without being stoned to death. Women in the West can have as many sexual partners as they have the time and will for.

Marriage is no longer the crowning achievement, and in some cultures its avoidance has resulted in the decline not only in the sex ratios of men to women, but in the entire population.

My son-in-law is Japanese. His brother, Masayuki, is married to Motoko. Motoko had a good job at Tokyo Electric. She put off marriage for ten years while Masayuki courted and pled and worked. Motoko told him she did not want to marry because, as a Japanese woman, she would have to give up her job to follow him to each new assignment—which meant moving every two to three years. Multiply that dynamic by a hundred million and you see that marriage to the young westernized Japanese woman is not the crowning glory of her womanhood, it is a punishment.

Deep in the biology of marriage, which is a legal state riding on a deep flow of genetic fitness, you see the flaws and the weaknesses of repressive thinking.

As culture has matured and transformed, humans are still running on Paleolithic legs. The result is a loosening of marriage as a cultural and social *sine qua non* and the return to the more true and more biological extended mating.

In a sense, humans have returned to their Deep-Time roots, and like the swan, can mate for life without the need of any blessing. Marriage as it evolves has left its trappings in the dust. But what happens when a woman says no?

The "no" is a statement of the evolved female. The male reaction is usually to demonize the woman and, not being satisfied with "no," impose himself on her. That is rape and as rape it violates the essence of sexual selection.

Choice is the word. Women choose. Men have to meet the demand of choice—they are chosen.

In the lekking species, such as sage grouse and Bowerbirds, males mark out a small patch of ground called a lek. In a flock of sage grouse, the males dance. They dance, they thump the ground of the lek and they puff out their breasts till they look like balloons. The male who lasts—the last male standing—gets chosen. He is chosen for his beauty, his stamina, his body, his fat, his resources, and his strength. The female chooses. Always, the female chooses.

Musth in the male elephant.

In musth, the male catches the pheromonal scent of the female. She runs, he chases her. On the chase, he develops green penis—an erection several feet long dripping with green exudate. After the run, the female chooses the male if he is still standing. The male *is chosen*. He does not choose, he is chosen for his beauty, his resource, and his strength.

Marriage isn't a question here. Musth is a temporary interruption that allows the male to spew his paltry two hundred billion sperm in hopes that one of them will skewer an ovum and his genes will be launched into the future.

From DeVore's words regarding sexual selection, "Males are basically a breeding experiment run by females," he draws this truth—"Males are the safest, most consistent way to contribute variation to the system . . ."

In the West, marriage is now more a cultural display along the lines of a potlatch to show wealth in lieu of a bride price or a dowry. In contemporary America, a wedding can cost upwards of fifty thousand dollars for a marriage likely to last only a few years. In this, we see the Western female settling into serial polygamy—once, twice, thrice. Marriage, in the twenty-first century, isn't a biological imperative interrupted by social and cultural dicta. The wisdom of marriage in the West is to measure cultural and social changes and the causal or resultant case of the biologically free woman choosing.

THE WISDOM OF SEX

I've been writing about the irrelevance of most of what I know. I've explored my education to discover its redundancy in a world that isn't anchored. I've delved into the obsolescence of temporal wisdom to find that in time, most of what I call wisdom is useless. There is a temporal aspect to wisdom and there is a temporal aspect to knowledge. And there is that overriding carnal aspect. Most of what I know passed into history long ago. I've been working on the wisdom of silence to see what that means and have come to the idea that knowing what to say and when to say it are not as important as knowing when to keep silent. You do not say that one comment which destroys all of what you have built. But how do you ever know?

How do you know that you're in that moment? There are so many homophones in English. The wisdom of homophones lets you control the image that emerges when you hear the word "road," and then in context see that the word is "rode." Until you are in the moment of the unraveling, you do not know which word was the destructor.

This is a puzzle of sorts because it forces you to recognize that no word by itself means anything. In the lexicon, each word is defined by other words. And so it is with the silent moment—at any moment, all meanings are potential. The potential for wisdom, then, in relationship means that at every moment, you carry all the history and all the previous moments, and in that context, as with a single word, you define each moment in terms of the previous and emerging moments.

In that moment, you measure the power of silence and in that moment, you know what not to say. It is, therefore, hurtful if you speak when silence tells you silence is best. I have seen many instances of this—saying to the loved one the one thing that taps into the sting with its hurt.

Let us say your loved one leaves a toothpick on the dinner plate. You dine together three hundred and sixty-five days a year. But on the three hundred and sixty-third day, you say, "I hate it when you leave your toothpick on the plate." Tears. Why?

In any moment are buried all previous moments and all possible moments, and in that moment you realize that it is not the toothpick you are seeing but the cigarette the father stubbed out in his plate of bacon and eggs. Your anguish is attached to the father and has nothing to do with that toothpick on your loved one's plate.

Those three hundred and sixty-two toothpicks.

You have not examined your own life and because you have not, you bring agony into the world. Wisdom is knowing what to say as well as when to say it. Is wisdom, then, a way to ease our agony?

The wisdom not to say, "Why do you do that?" is the wisdom of permanence unless you set out to hurt; then, there is no wisdom, only cruelty.

I want to write about the wisdom of sex. The wisdom of sex is a touchy topic, but it is a real topic because there is no person on earth who is not the result of sex. There are two topics worth writing about—sex and death.

The French call orgasm, *la petite mort*. The little death. Science and neurology have told us that, in fact, at the moment of orgasm, male or female, we lose consciousness. We are in a sense, dead, but in the aftermath of orgasm, we return, and in returning find again the pleasure that came just before *la petite mort*. Somewhere, sometime, humans decided that life had to be a decision, not an accident—to replace reproductive sex with recreational sex. We know from the archaeologists and the anthropologists who study Elizabethan toilets that the detritus is loaded with sheep intestine condoms. We know that condoms are called French letters, so we know that recreational sex has a long history. We know that the Romans understood the relationship between sex and offspring and often chose to avoid the latter by using a number of devices to control the fate of semen. The wisdom of sex has at least two sides—knowing that, we also know that in the Arab world there is a saying: "I'd rather hear a fat boy fart than a cute girl sing."

Sex is a multiplicity.

Humans have discovered ways to avoid pregnancy, and we know from the Saxons of the Anglo-Saxons that a bit of brown does not entail sugar.

Wisdom of sex has a catalog of means, and as we continue to explore the range from procreation to recreation we also discover a range of sexes.

In the beginning, there was one male and one female. This is the evolutionary reality. Out of the two came a third. And then, the opportunity for reality to change occurred. There are not just two sexes—there are at least four: man/woman, lesbian/gay. The range increases until there are six, then eight, then twenty.

Sex and gender become a fine point in the wisdom of sex. Sex and sexuality become points with sex and gender. In the end, as psychologist Jarvis Bastian told us, "It is amazing how many of us are under the bell."

Given the infinite possibilities for chaos in recombinant DNA, the wisdom of sex has to have its own moment.

So, I brush over it here.

In the dictionary of the possible, we have just begun to define.

Today, I also intended to write about the wisdom of "stupid." Earlier I asked if there is a stupid wisdom. Do stupid people know they are stupid? Is there a wisdom of stupidity? I don't know, but I do know this: If men clip their toenails, grind them into powder, and eat the powder, will the powder in fact give a man the same powerful erection he thinks he gets from ground-up pangolin scale or powdered rhino horn? Thousands of pangolins are murdered every year so that a man can, by magic, enlarge his penis and its erection. Why murder pangolins? Why slaughter rhinos? Why not just clip your fingernails and eat the powder? Keratin is keratin, if it comes from a rhino horn, a pangolin, or a man's toenails. Are all the "old folk remedies" examples of stupid wisdom? Is it wisdom to eat tiger penis to cure erectile disfunction?

A definition bears on the question of wisdom: If wisdom is knowledge and if wisdom is experience and if wisdom with its knowledge can be passed on, then it stands to reason that stupid people who do not know they are stupid are passing on their stupid wisdom to their children. That explains Donald Trump. It explains Mario Rubio. It explains why a man eats bulls' testicles to enhance his sexual prowess. And, of course, it explains Ted Cruz, Mitch McConnell, and every impotent Republican in politics who thinks that murdering an elephant makes him a real man. Stupid wisdom. Vestigial superstition in the age of DNA genomics and polymers.

If wisdom is a kind of universal statement about how to avoid pain and death, how to build a culture out of experience, and how to ease our agony, then the stupid people are busy building a stupid culture based on guns, racism, anger, too little recreational sex, and too much powdered pangolin scale.

Someone has to tell them to stop having kids, to stop passing on their stupidity, to stop getting in the way of progress, to stop eating tiger penis.

But without the stupidity of people, how do we measure progress?

What is progress?

Is progress the distance we have traveled from stone tools to hydrogen bombs? From caves to palaces? From procreative sex to recreational sex?

Progress is a measure of our scientific understanding of the world, and without the science, we know nothing but what we are told, only what we do. We are stupid people passing on stupidity as wisdom.

So, I think that the wisdom of stupidity is an oxymoron. You cannot be both stupid and wise. As I explore the case for wisdom, I come to stopping points. I have to read and understand what came before so that I have some sense of what to pass on. In procreative sex, all we pass on is DNA. Genes.

In recreational sex, we pass on nothing except STDs and HIV, but it is not the purpose of wisdom to pass on our illnesses. Knowing what to pass on and what to take to the grave is the essence of wisdom. There is the silence of doing nothing, as well.

At some point, we understand that to pass on culture, we need a store of knowledge about the world and what we are doing in it. Just as the first chemists were cooks, so the first sociologists were men and women who learned about their world and then told their offspring about that learning. But as we have proliferated nigh unto oblivion in the modern world, what we need to know to keep the culture alive has broadened, leaving us bereft of what to teach.

I do not know right now what I would do if asked to design a course in culture and civilization for my grandchildren. I am aggrieved by my own ignorance.

MARCH 1

WISDOM AND THE WHEEL

In my novel, *Trio of Lost Souls*, Jim Garret tells Vincent that he sat at the table in the water tower for years waiting for wisdom to come to him, but it never came.

Wisdom, it seems, isn't something you wait for, it is something you have to search for. But how do you do that?

Wisdom has a temporal aspect—what I know today will be of no use to anyone tomorrow.

Wisdom has this aspect of obsolescence—what works today will not work tomorrow.

Wisdom has an aspect of irrelevance. The things I know to be true, to be exact, things that I know work, will be irrelevant to the next generation that has to invent its own wheels. All wheels are round, but if you say, "Try this, do this, or this," the young around you say, "Your way kills my creativity," and then they produce a wheel. They call it a story, a poem, a novel, a screenplay, but it is always a wheel, just like every other wheel. It is round.

Wisdom in its deeper way has an aspect of redundancy.

What is being done, what is being seen, what is being created has already been done, has already been seen, has already been created, time and time again. The redundancy of wisdom is astounding, but for the key few devices that change the world.

I have read the *Meditations* of Marcus Aurelius—a man who at the height of his power was the most powerful man in the world. I learned from Marcus that his wisdom has a kind of permanence to it. A question remains: Would his wisdom exist had he not written it down? And moreover, would it exist if other writers had not taken him in to preserve his writing?

Marcus is a stoic. He doesn't get florid or arcane. He states that we as human beings have one obligation, and that is to community.

Death, Marcus writes, is the end. There is no soul, there is nothing after death. Death, he writes, is the equalizer. All humans die, and in dying, return to Nature, and Nature is the beginning and the end.

As I read Marcus, I saw his materialism in full flower, and I could think only of the eighteenth-century thinkers—the *philosophes*, the encyclopedists who knew that nothing was ever lost. They knew that all things on this planet live in a closed system called Earth along with all other creatures, and each and every one of them ends the same way. But nothing is ever destroyed; it only changes shape.

Solid flows into gas flows into liquid. Liquid returns to earth, Earth is solid again, and so it is with man and all living things.

The two lessons I learned from Marcus are, even as I write this, irrelevant to the young, who are reinventing their own wheel as they live through their own idealism with its canon of change and progress. But the wisdom of Marcus has its obsolete character as well. He fluctuates between the use of the word "God" with its "G" and "gods" with the small "g."

Nothing is fixed in his world except death and the return to nature.

As I wrote this, I time-traveled, using my prefrontal cortex, to the eighteenth century and to the Marquis de Sade. In Sade, I see this—murder destroys nothing but the ego. The I. The Me. The dead return to Earth, transformed as flowers and trees. So what is murder? The Marquis, in his quest, asks some terrifying questions.

What are any of the social conventions if nothing really vanishes?

In the Marquis' wisdom, there is disruption and there is chaos that leaves a deep wound in the human psyche. The death of millions at the hands of the few reveals the obsolescence of the Marquis, because his wisdom, pushed to the extreme, is at its root, only pain and agony. If murder doesn't matter, then why does it matter?

It must because of the value of The One. Each and every One in the Anthropocene is measurable and measured as worthy. Death with pain cannot be abided. In this, there is confusion of great sweep. In this, there is some aspect of choice. When human beings were small in number, there was no choice. Women had babies, babies grew into girls who became women, these women had more babies. There was no choice. But now, there is choice.

For the first time in memory, there is choice to void the biological imperative and in voiding the imperative, women have the choice to reproduce or not.

Materialism and stoicism run up against existentialism and the biology of desire. What is desire?

If you remove the biological imperative, what is desire?

If desire is the working out of the biological imperative with its insistent denial of choice, then what is desire?

If you remove procreative sex from the mix, you are left with recreational sex and the residue of desire is the anti-choice working in the body. Desire is the urge, even the drive to possess and be possessed. In *Citadel*, Trisha discovers that her need to be possessed changes in nature and act when the object of desire isn't a mere Y chromosome carrier, an ambulatory sperm donor, a sperm donor with an inflatable DNA injection tube. A man.

Desire is independent of the object of desire, and Trisha finds herself making love to Kel, a fictional daughter of the Citadel, in a time of no males, in a time of complete choice—and the choice is whether or not to allow the male of the species to go extinct.

But, then, Trisha has to ask the question: "What is a human?"

If, as Lynn Margulis writes, "sex is merely the exchange of genes," then what does Trisha feel when she makes love to the fictional Kel? If women can parthenogenetically produce offspring, and if "human" has been defined as the Y gamete fertilizing the X gamete to produce either an XY or an XX—what is a human?

Are parthenogenetic offspring human?

If there are not forty-six chromosomes, is the body human?

This is the question of desire linked to the question of defining a human being.

At its root, desire is a need to feel at one. Desire is the urge in the loins that makes the body crave touch. But touch is biologically linked to the exchange of DNA. Desire without the exchange of DNA has to be redefined.

Desire drives everything in humans—need drives desire in humans—love drives need in humans.

Trisha, the questioning protagonist of *Citadel*, tells Rose as she sits at an open window overlooking the Pacific Ocean that she hates being automatic. "I am an automatic being driven by desire to the beach to find a sweaty bloody man to fertilize one of my eggs."

In *Citadel*, Trisha confronts her own automatism as she acknowledges the residual evolutionary responses that define and drive her. She attains, by reading Daiva's novel, the wisdom of desire, and she learns that by attaining desire she has to make choices. If it is desire driving her, then desire doesn't have to be penetration or possession. Desire can be something beyond but inescapably biological.

If all of our knowledge is nothing but an elaborate attempt to deny biology, then what are we?

MARCH 4

THE WISDOM OF MYTH

Today, I have no idea why I am here at the table pretending to be a writer. Why write at all? There is no need any more for words on the page or the images hidden in the words or the actions lurking behind the verbs.

As I read more about the brain and how it evolved, the more I see that our brain, the human brain, is so pliable and pliant that it might not be anything at all but a device to let us see what we want to see, to see what we expect to see, to see what we need to see, and, most important of all, to ignore what we cannot bear to see.

Selective blindness.

In a sense, as the brain evolved, it brought with it everything we need to know. In the structure of the brain there is embedded already all the characters, all the plots, and what we learn from writers, such as C.G. Jung and Claude Lévi-Strauss, is that we simply cloak characters and plots in some temporal garb. In the end, all things are already done and said, so what is "creative" writing? Re-storytelling. Nothing more.

Fiction is an exercise in clothing. It is an exercise in time. And, in a way, this notion, borrowed from C.G. Jung and Ferdinand de Saussure and Lévi-Strauss, tells us why in the modern world writing about the self in time represents a shift in the world as we see it.

As I explore the writing of today, I look not at the story—the story will be a static or dynamic retelling of the original myths that all stories are based on, the archetypes, character, or journey. What is important to me is to learn how the writer did it. I know the story, but what is the structure? What is the style? What is the idiolect of the writer?

In the past, writers and thinkers such as Propp, in *Morphology of the Folktale*, while telling us that the core stories, having come down with the evolving brain, leave no chance for creativity or invention, also suggest that the writing world has fallen into a pit of self-adoration bequeathing us a plethora of how-to-love-ourselves books which, at the root, tell us nothing that can't already be found in Elias Canetti's *Crowds and Power*.

Or in Jung's *The Archetypes and the Collective Unconscious*.

Or Lévi-Strauss' *Mythologies*.

All of the writing of books leads to imitation. It is curious that in a world that gives us the computer with its infinite possibilities, all writing is locked into a finite set of *remakes*.

The remake does two things: It re-cloaks the original myth, and that tells us that writing is dead.

I tell a story—a man from a shipwreck lands on an island where he meets a savage who just happens to know the cult of nature. The Savage teaches the Castaway about nature. And seeing this, readers say "Ah! *Robinson Crusoe*."

Wrong, I say. I'm telling you the story of *The Architect and the Emperor of Assyria*, which is a retelling of *The Tempest*, just as is Crusoe. That leaves us with the film, *Cast Away*, where the modern world meets the emptiness of the remake—where the character on that island talks not to a savage who would have the secrets of the universe but to a volleyball.

In this, the writer comes to grips with the vacuum of the modern world. The myths no longer yield allegory. Allegory has died, and the emptiness leads into the total democratization of the mind where, as Asimov wrote—"Your ignorance is as important as my knowledge." Here, science dies. Creativity dies.

The dilemma for the modern writer is this: What do I write about if I am an ignorant, unread, scientifically stupid person? There is one thing left to write about—the self.

So often, now, I hear people say, "that movie isn't anything new, it feels familiar, it's not what is happening."

In the writing world, all of the writing of books leads down the path of imitation. At the core, every story rests on a myth told and retold until it becomes as bland as the writing major publishers demand, writing slimmed down, pared down, dumbed down as if by slicing away the body, the bones will be enough.

In this new poverty of the mind, the writer writes about the self.

The others who surround and punish and mangle the self and the psyche leave the wounded to pose as writers who do not have the infrastructure of mind to release the myths that they would imitate.

It is all so familiar. Everything stays the same, except language. Language, our meager attempt to explore emotion with words.

All mysteries and detective novels are shadows of one another. All romance novels teach the same lesson of love with these two transformations—happiness or tragedy, love and loss. Repetition after repetition.

As the writing of books grows in number, the number of writers who fail as writers grows, and out of that failure comes disdain, with reason.

The veil has been lifted. The wizard is naked. His truth is known.

"This has all happened before and it will all happen again." One of the great and final truths and observations that writers of the remake of *Battlestar Galactica* made, and in that remake, *Battlestar Galactica* becomes a metafiction in which the writers summarize all previous stories with "this has all happened before and it will all happen again." As the ancients said, there is nothing new under the sun—*nihil sub sole novum.*

We are destined to an infinite number of repetitions of our repetitions of the myths that came down with the brain, including as it did all previous experience as in the parasympathetic and the sympathetic nervous system. Some things we react to—we flee, we blink, our breath increases as our heart beats faster, and, in the brain, the mirror neurons mimic action, the mirrors of the actual world encoded in the brain to bring the same reaction to an infinite number of viewers.

It is in the dark room of the mind that the repetition takes place and the body reacts as all animals have reacted and will react. The brain is not individual but a collective accretion of all past experience, and in the darkness the stories are born. All of the stories are the same to all the brains that experience them.

As I read Marcus Aurelius' *Meditations*, I wondered at how this man, a Roman emperor at the apogee of Roman power, could write that nature is all. We are born, we live, and we return to nature. All of us go back into the same darkness.

Marcus did not write allegory and he did not write metaphor. His experience, his living told him the utter truth: There is nothing beyond, there is only the now, and in the now, there is only the body. In this rejection of metaphor, Marcus tells us the truth that even now we choose not to accept. He told us that this has happened before and it will happen again. Marcus wrote two thousand years ago what the writers of *Battlestar Galactica* wrote early in the twenty-first century.

And there is a lesson in this.

As I read the moderns, I see in them the myths clad in time, in costume, and as time has dilated, I have seen the costumes change, the hats change, the dresses change, the shoes and coats all change. The one thing that has not changed is the myth bases, and we have just about written them to death. We have emptied ourselves of meaning.

We have written them as far as they will go.

And, in this hiatus of invention, we have only the self to write about.

In Marcus' *Meditations*, he writes to the "you," but in the reading, you know he is writing to and for himself. His work is an exploration of a man in time and space facing his mortality. It has happened before and it will happen again.

This is something we all do. We invent religion to deal with mortality. We invent gods who can give us immortality. But for all that, as Marcus writes, we go back into the darkness whence we came and the Other comes to take our place. The Other dons new costumes and new shoes but his brain carries the same myths we carried before we died. He invents his own world, only to find that it has all happened before and it will all happen again and again and again.

This is the writer's dilemma.

The catalog is limited, the outcome is always the same, the purpose is always the same, the lexicon might differ but its goal is always the same. It is the fate of the writer to learn that there is no invention because the brain already has its built-in residual evolutionary responses and the mirror neurons can only reflect the myths that came with the brain.

In Marcus' writing, we come face-to-face with the Roman idea of the closed system they adopted from the Greeks. Materialism is at the foundation of science. In our closed system, matter is never destroyed, it is only transformed. Lavoisier codified what Marcus already knew.

MYTH IN THE MIND

Does the wisdom of silence shape up to be the root of all wisdom? What to say and when to say it. What not to say. How to keep silent is the Tao of the mind, a silence that has both depth and girth but holds itself away. Silence is invisible.

Deep in the discussion of wisdom, I came to the wisdom of myth. The question I pose here is: "Where is myth in the mind?"

Another question is this: "Will children who are not taught a mythology of being still have myth in the mind?"

Mind is what brain does. Eric Kandel writes that he wanted to be a psychiatrist and as a psychiatrist find the place in the brain where the Freudian structures lived. "Where," for example, he asked, "is the id? Where is the ego? Where is the super ego?"

Kandel writes that as he explored the brain he did not find a locus for the id, the ego, or the super ego. From that experience he writes that these things are nowhere in the brain but are constructs of the mind; the mind is what the brain does and so there is no locus, for they are process.

Mind. Process of the brain. Into this comes the question of myth. Is myth also a process and a construct of the brain? Myth is nowhere but it is somewhere, and as I watch writers uncover story after story, I see myth emerging from the writing.

It is a super-segmental structure without form, just as Jung describes the archetypes. You cannot see an archetype, but you can see the temporal aspect of the archetype in the time of the writer. So, again, the question, "do children not raised with a mythology have an inherent myth?"

The question also appears, "do children who have no learning or experience have an id, an ego, and a super ego?" If these things are processes of the brain, then they are inherent in the brain but nowhere present in pure form—that is, in experiential reality—as isolated from behavior built into behavior as aspects of personality.

The questions that suggest themselves, then: "do all humans have ego and superego? Is that the doing of the brain?" We know that all humans have innate myth. The story that appears as myth is built on the non-evident archetype that appears not as a conscious reality but as a form that escapes from the mind in time and space dressed in clothing that temporalizes the archetype.

Both Jung and Neumann write that there is a Mother archetype. All humans come from a mother. The physical mother exists for only a short time and then disappears. But the archetypal mother is buried in the brain and its processes, and she comes out in time, clothed in time, and eternal in story. A writer must deal with this reality.

When Jung first read about the Aztec ceremony of the corn cakes, he was struck with how similar the process of postulants devouring the god in the form of a corn cake was to the Christian devouring the body of Christ in the sacramental wafer. "This act," Jung writes, "shows the perpetual reality of the symbol and the residual archetype—the postulant eats the god who has died but is reborn in the archetypal mythic pattern. The mythic pattern," Jung asserts, "cannot be the result of cultural cross contamination, but must be the result of the mind and what it carries through time. The wisdom of myth perpetuates itself and cries out for an answer to the question, will children untaught have myth in the mind?"

The answer, at best a guess, is "yes."

If mind is a process of brain, and if all humans have the same structures of brain, then the process of brain called mind will produce identical mythic structures.

When Claude Lévi-Strauss went to the Amazon to be with the forest people, he was struck with the archetypal perpetuation of the mythic structures and their stories—their myths—that he had seen and described in other mythologies.

The wisdom of myth, then, is what binds mind to mind. Claude Lévi-Strauss, as did Jung, sees that the teaching is possible because myth is already there. But where is it? What can we learn from it? What do we do with it?

It is known that every story has a myth base. The myth base doesn't have to be a myth known to the reader, the listener, the viewer. In the telling, the mind of each strips away the temporal aspects of the story and the myth stands naked in its archetypes. Naked and taken into mind through brain processes linking human mind to human mind. Natalie Goldberg writes that writing is mind connecting to mind. Mind does connect to mind and the linkages are independent of the myth of the story because mind connects myth to myth and archetype to archetypal structure.

The pattern persists. The persistence of myth must somehow be accounted for through science.

There are three stories in every story. First there is the story that the ego, that is, the "I," wants credit for. "I wrote the story to make me famous." Then, there is the archetypal story embedded in mind that wants to be told, and that story belongs to no one. It is pure story. Third is the story the reader/listener/viewer wants and expects to be told. When the second and third stories are not in sync, the artist loses contact and the myth is lost.

When the writer reveals the myth base, the reader connects. In each of their archetypes, Attis, Adonis, Christ, and Osiris are identical. The god dies and is reborn. When Jung encountered the Mesoamerican myths, he found that their archetypes persisted. He added the name of the "corn god of the Aztecs" to the quartet of names.

How does the writer reveal the myth base?

The myth base is revealed as structure and parallels. In *The Manchurian Candidate*, the author reveals the myth base in this way: Capt. Marco and Raymond Shaw are celebrating Christmas by drinking wine. Shaw is very drunk. He has complained about his mother—he hates her, he says, but he tells Marco, "You don't want to hear me complain about my mother."

"Oh no," Marco says. "Hearing you complain about your mother is like listening to Orestes complain about Clytemnestra."

With that analogy, the author reveals the myth base and it is this: A decorated war hero returns home—archetypal pattern—to find that his mother has murdered his father—the archetypes mother/father—and she is living with her lover Aegisthus—the archetypal lover—and the hero kills both the mother and the lover to avenge the father.

In *The Oresteia*, Orestes, Clytemnestra, Aegisthus, and Agamemnon match point-for-point Raymond Shaw with his stepfather in *The Manchurian Candidate*. Shaw kills both mother and lover. This revelation persists whether the writer is conscious of it or not. It is interesting to note that in the novel, *The Manchurian Candidate*, the myth base is implied but never stated. Still, the archetypal pattern is there in all its mythic completeness. One writer implies, the other states directly.

Myth persists and myth base is mind connecting to mind. Even if the reader does not know the exact myth, the structure is there.

This is the wisdom of myth. Myth connects us one to another and it needs to answer the question, "is there a myth base to personal writing?"

Most personal writing is about family. In family, there are a minimum of three archetypes—mother, father, child.

Family is the foundation of all personal writing, and in the writing, the writer cloaks the archetype in dress and time. Despite the clothing, every reader sees the structure.

The reader does not need to know the name of the mother because in mind connecting to mind, mother connects to mother, myth connects to myth, archetype connects to archetype.

The untaught reader/viewer must have archetypal mythic structures as patterns of mind. All personal writing tells the story of the good mother, the story of the wicked stepmother, or the story of the death Crone. These archetypes are instantly recognizable.

MARCH 18

IN THE BEGINNING WHEN NOT EVERYONE WROTE

Why do we write? Why are we a "writing culture?"

There are cultures where the writing is done by a few. Some, in the past, where the writing was done by a cultish few—the priests, the scribes, the scholars.

In the West, to be literate—to write, to read—is a part of being in the culture. To be true to the culture, you write.

In Digital Age America, writing has become something else. When, as in the wisdom of myth, the core has died and with it, its death story, there is nothing left to write about but the self. As Americans release writing and, with it, reading, writing returns to its cultish origin in which the code is digital and the product is image.

In the beginning, not everyone wrote.

In the beginning, writing was tedious, difficult, obscure. As we enter the second century of the Age of Images, writing, once again, is done by a few. In the Age of Images, we, the aficionados of not just the fixed image but the moving image, we see writing going dark. Author Dennis Must, in his letters to me, explains that "going dark" is a theatrical term. Lights down. Curtain closed. Dark. Dennis further explains that we are in the final stages of the Gutenbergian world where the book as physical object disappears, while in the digital world we now live in, behind every moving image, there is a line of digital code. It can be a script, it can be a computer-graphic line of code, it can be an improvised dance, but behind every image, every moving image, there is code and that code is not in words. It is in bytes, electrons. The image itself does not exist until the high priests of the electron turn the code into image.

Why do I write words? Why do we write words?

The easy answer is—"because we have to."

All writers suffer from a compulsion to write, but saying "because I have to" is not an explanation or an exploration of the root; it is a cliché.

Writing words, I think, pleases a deep and obscure urge. Writing meets a profound biological need. Writing, like any experience, can reconfigure the brain. The act of writing words that have not been read before, writing a poem that has not been written before, creating an image that did not exist before—in that writing, the brain builds itself just as muscle builds with exercise to reconfigure the body.

We are shape-shifters.

We can balloon to enormous size, we can shrink to a shadow, and we can transform into a mesomorphic being with flat belly, enormous thighs, and sculpted biceps.

As with the body, so is the brain. Writing builds upon itself, and as the brain's neurons and axons and dendritic nexus strengthen, the brain becomes more lithe, more supple, more muscular. At one level, I write to keep my brain alive. But I know that mind is what brain does. Is it possible that writing to reconfigure my brain also builds more mind?

There is no place, no locus in the brain where the mind resides. Unlike the amygdala, where perception goes to be sorted into long-term or short-term memory, there is no single place in the brain where mind dwells. But mind is the process of brain, and so all of brain is all of mind. The writer has mind, and in writing brings sentences out into the world that have not been inscribed into any other mind, anywhere.

Jarvis Bastian, an admired professor at UC Davis, once told me that no two sentences can ever be identical. If I ask you to repeat what I say, he told me, you repeat the words but not the intention. Each aspect of mind is different. My intention was to tell you to repeat it. From Jarvis's explanation of uniqueness, I understand that writing is the willful production of intention through words.

As we write, we grow. No two sentences can ever be exact replicas. I write to exercise my mind. To write words is to drop into the greatest human social experiment of all time that derives from the greatest evolutionary development of all time—the cerebral cortex.

The cortex, which in its mystery is greater than the creation of the universe, can not only refer to its own creation but also can travel in time—back and forth. As it travels, it engages the mirror neurons that leave the body feeling that it is experiencing the act of travel.

The mirror neurons explain all of writing, all of storytelling, all of everything, because as you read, you experience the brain decoding words into images, images that move, images that leave you feeling that you are doing what the words are doing. It is an illusion of brain feeding into mind because you have not moved a muscle except for the orbital muscles that move the eyes, yet you experience the passion and the agony, you feel the sexual mystery, and you "imagine" the pain of the knife piercing the flesh. We write, it seems, so that we may experience the lives of others without leaving our chairs.

The brain drives the mind that feasts on the lives that do not exist except in written words, yet how the words decode their meaning is a mystery the brain has yet to let us see. The brain is more than an amalgam of neurons, axons, synapses, and ganglia. The brain is the instrument that writes about itself as it brings others to write what they think and dream. How is that possible?

What lies beyond the brain? Is it possible that the world we see is a construct of the brain and what we see is not there but merely a reality-of-mind that the brain constructs in its need to make sense of perception?

This argument returns us to the eighteenth century, when the question about reality was brought again out of the classical mind into the mind of the Enlightenment.

Lévi-Strauss has written that human beings have *always*, emphasis on "always," thought well, but we have not always thought technologically. The brain lets us write and create a world both efficient and sufficient. In its efficiency, there is no need for more. But at other times, sufficient is not enough, and, as if the brain has rested for millennia, it then asks more of experience to integrate into mind. That integration lifts the species into new domains. Once stimulated, the questioning brain is insatiable: dissatisfied and eager for more.

In that questioning, the reconfiguring is done. The brain changes. With these changes, the mind is no longer satisfied with the efficient, sufficient model it has built. We see this in the lacunae of time—"for a thousand years."

"The Empire lived in peace for five hundred years."

But then the walls crack, the interstices widen, the cerebral gyri are no longer comfortable, and a revolution begins. And it all came from writing.

As Pascal writes, "*combien de royaumes nous ignorent.*" How many realms ignore us. Realms we know nothing about. And then a question is asked, "What lies beyond?" The answer to that question is the rhythm of change: Stasis. Expansion. Stasis.

There have been cultures that did not write. Of them, nothing is known but the hard and the durable. A wall built of mud dissolves in rain. A wall built of stone does not. The stones that remain tell us what the dead did but they do not tell us how they did it or why.

We can only infer, using that marvel of evolution—the cerebral cortex—what they must have done. For a few minutes, we stand in their shoes, inventing a reality that does not exist except in our hunger to know and in the brain's need to construct reality. We build a story around the stones, and the words we use are "must have" and "probably lived" and "it is possible that." Our brain needs to construct the past so that the present makes sense, and this need is why we write—to dig up the past, to give the *now* an immediate meaning. We write about the *past*—the past itself, the self's experience of *then*, to understand the reality the "I" lives in *today*.

We write a continuous story about ourselves—as a race and as individuals of the race. The brain, it seems, is trying to understand itself in time to see how it got here. And it needs to know.

We have offspring so our brain passes to the next phase. The brain, in its urgency to understand what brought it here, goes on an endless quest to understand, not just the past but also its future.

MARCH 22

THE WISDOM OF TOOLS: THE MASON

Today, I'm writing about work.

About the wisdom of work.

About the wisdom of the workingman.

About the man and the work.

The workingman works with his hands, he works with his tools, and he knows the tools.

In his tools, you see his wisdom. He knows what to do. He knows how to do it. He knows when to do it. And the tools, his tools, are sacred to him as he uses them.

Sacred because without them he can't do what needs to be done. The tools in the hands of a workingman tell him when and where and how and for whom.

The mason arrives at 8:30 a.m. His truck is a tool that carries all of his tools—but most important is the man. The man who knows the tools, which tools to use, and when to use them. The wisdom is not in the tools but in the man.

The tools let us see the man as he works. He knows how and when and why.

He has brought a ladder. He has brought a mixer for the concrete. He has brought the right power tool.

"Power?" he asks me at 8:35.

I point to the power outlet on the lamppost by the driveway.

"And water?" he says to me.

I show him the spigots still under their winter caps.

"All right to mix here? I won't leave a mess."

Then, from the truck comes the tools—the power cord, the grinder, the hoses, the trowels and scrapers, the chisels and the hammer. All the tools laid out. Tools. Without the tools, what is the man? What are we?

He lays out the stainless steel chimney cap, the sheen of the steel dulled by the mist of the morning. The chimney cap, a tool he knows how to use, and why.

It is not enough to be. You must be wise. Wisdom is always knowing what to do, and when to do it, and why to do it. But it is more than knowing. There is more to wisdom than simply knowing. I think about the story of the railroad worker whose job was to tap the steel wheels of the railcars at the station.

But no one told him why.

Why tap the steel wheels?

Clanging, he walked the length of the train—why? Why tap the wheels? No one told him to listen for the dull thud of cracked steel. A man with a tool—the hammer—but not knowing why, knowing only what.

So wisdom is just not what, but why and when and how.

The man on the roof transforms from a man to half a machine as he dons his breather—a tool that he knows will keep him safe and alive.

The man with the mask starts his grinder—it is a durable instrument, a precision instrument that he uses to grind out the rotten grout, grout weathered by rain and ice and snow and heat until the bricks loosen.

And, there is dust.

The mask, the life-giving and lifesaving breather is sheathed in a cloud of dust—mortar dust—ground so fine it flies and fills the air and settles in the house.

Tools.

Every tool as precise as the man.

Minutes and hours slide by before the grinding falls silent. Then, comes the hammering. The sound of hammer and chisel. The sound of brick and steel and concrete—the mask, the grinder. The hammer and the chisel now laid aside.

Silence, as the man hoists the buckets filled with sand and cement and water mixed in a mixer that until this moment has lain at the ready—with the tool, the trowel. The man fills the gaps that he ground around the brick and builds the stack. He builds the stack with thin brick he has cut with the saw, and he lays the brick onto the bed of grout and you hear the *tap-tap-tapping* of the handle of the trowel on the brick. When the cap is sealed and the mortar set, the man locks the shiny steel chimney cap in place and the sun blazes from it, stabbing the eye with its solar sharpness. He steps back for a look at his work.

The work of a man with tools. The right tools for the right job at the right time. He is done. The work is done. He knows the work is done.

He has done it many times, for many days, for many people, and his wisdom is knowing when to do it, why to do it, and when it is done.

The mason works with his hands in the sun and the wind. His work is smooth and well done, and his work, were it a man, would be proud. The work would tell him, "Terry, you do magnificent work. And I am happy and I am proud to see this work done so well." That is what I tell him now.

Has no one ever told him before that his work is superior? Has no one told him that he, with his tools, has cleaned out the rot, saved the decaying corpse of time in the brick and the moss and the grit?

He blushes. This man blushes, and I know that always before the recompense was only money. They pay him for his time, for his body, for his tools. But more than that, they pay him for what he knows. He knows what he sees when he sees it and he reads the palm of time and weather and he knows he can fix the ruined and ragged residue of time—that is what he does.

But cash is not enough.

I know it is not enough.

I have worked with my hands and gotten only cash. I have sweated in the fields and groaned in the packing sheds and I have hurt my hands, my body working in tunnels. The cash is never enough.

I know it is not enough. That is why I tell the man with the tools that his work is fine work, well done. But the wisdom of work, like all wisdom, is temporal. There'll be a time when the mason will not go onto the roof with his tools because what he knows will no longer be needed.

Steel and glass will take the place of brick and grout, and the man's wisdom will die with him. The wisdom of work will be silent and there will be no one to pass the knowledge to. Yes, wisdom is knowing what to do, when to do it, why to do it, and the last, the very last thing—knowing it is no longer needed.

So it is with this mason.

As I look at his work, I see the wisdom that hearkens back to a time when the laying of brick was an art.

You see it today in older places living past their time. You see rows of soldiers—the side-by-side, thin brick at attention—and you see the sailors wide and side-by-side. You see the courses stacked up, you see the art and the end of the mason's wisdom.

All his secrets will die the day those buildings come down.

He says to me, as he washes and dries his hands to flush away the remains of his craft, "Your chimney is over fifty years old. They don't do it that way anymore."

He points to the brick now capped with its stainless steel crown. "You see? These bricks aren't regular. These are four-inchers mixed with the two-inchers with the square bricks layered into rectangles. There is a name for that," he says, "but no one remembers it. The man who taught me—T Bolt—knew, but he did not tell me."

And, for a moment, I am sad. The waning of wisdom, the dying of an art. I am thankful that the mason sees the art of his predecessors, men who knew secrets that died with them.

He stands looking up at his work. It is solid work done by a solid man, a fine and good man. He smiles.

His tools are now back in the truck. The power cord and grinder, the hammer and the chisels, the buckets and the mixer are all now hidden in the belly of the truck.

It is with some regret that I hand the man with the tools a piece of paper with his reward on it. I know that his work will last far longer than the cash.

As he climbs into his truck, he says, "If you know anyone who needs their chimney tuck pointed, give them my number."

With regret, I watch the man, the workingman, the stonemason, drive away.

And then, in silence, I go back into my house, where the faint odor of fresh grout clings to the air, the scent of a timeless ritual.

MAY 1

THE ARROGANCE OF THE PRINCELY MIND

The princely mind, in its arrogance, knows nothing but itself. The only thing, to the princely mind, is the princely mind.

What is arrogance?

What is the princely mind?

How do you measure the arrogance of such a mind as the princely mind?

We live in an Age of Self. The Self devoid of its deities is a lost self at war with the common good. Stripped of its connections, the Self enters into a time of pure selfish existence.

With no bounds on its greed, without regard for the other, the princely mind takes itself to be divine. All others exist so the princely mind can achieve its goal of total possession of everything in existence.

In the last few decades of the twentieth century, we saw the Self elevated to a princely status where only the "I" mattered. All existence was filtered through the lens of the "I." This tendency flattened out the culture of the others.

In the culture of the others that is the culture of the past, it was incumbent upon each of us to think of the other while gathering for ourselves. In the past, we were encouraged and taught to think about the pain of the other, to see the anguish of loss, to understand what stamina of mind and being it took to stand on a corner, palm out, asking for alms.

Elevated to princely status through inheritance of wealth and assumptive greed, the princely mind does not see the ruin of civilization in the outstretched palm but sees only the worthlessness of that other. The princely mind imagines itself at the pinnacle of the world. And, in this insanity, there is destruction.

In extremis, the princely mind has no redeemer, has no hope, has no recourse, because in death, as in life, the only essence of existence is the Self, and so the princely mind laments itself, "poor me, I must live forever." The mirror of time reflects on his or her own anguish as if divorced from the entire spectrum of humanity. Yet, we all came out of Africa. We all, at one time, spoke one language.

In this time, we need to look not at philosophy, not at religion, but at biology to understand who and what we are. We must look to science for knowledge of how we came to be who we are and for the tools to understand how it is possible for the princely mind to distance itself from its own science of being.

What is the princely mind in this second decade of the twenty-first century? What is it if not the Self exalting itself at the expense of all others, at the cost of endless pain and the damage of greed? The princely mind's arrogance sets itself apart from the ebb and flow of evolution to find in its self-love, not the peace of no desire but the anguish of endless and insatiable and infinite greed.

The princely mind in its arrogance never asks how much is enough, but asks instead, how much more can I acquire?

The princely mind, then, is the apotheosis of greed and exemplifies the death of democracy in a flood of gold and silver and possessions and jewels. The princely mind is a desert of its own making, not the result of millennia of natural and sexual selection. It is an aberration, a distortion, a sickly mutation, a fraud.

In the Paleolithic era, women chose males for breeding based on three traits—speed, size, and aggression.

In this, the end of the Anthropocene, women choose males for breeding based on wealth, power, and position.

In the evolution of the princely mind, women are a reward, but the princely mind, ignorant of its own origins, believes that it, the arrogant mind, is the one choosing. In this assumption, the princely mind is a complete desert of ignorance, a field of emptiness surrounded by monuments to itself—all at the expense of others.

Eric Kandel writes in *The Age of Insight* that artists must learn to pay attention to the neurosciences. Writers, it seems, must also learn to pay attention to biology and desire.

Sigmund Freud knew that he did not know enough about biology to understand the human mind and its workings in its totality. He understood that all brains are the same, all driven by the same evolutionary energy, but he did not know why. He did not know the mechanisms. In his humility, Freud achieved a certain arrogance for which we can forgive him, because he knew the truth lay in the body as it had evolved. He knew that he did not know the truth, but anticipated it when he said that we are nothing but chemistry.

When Eric Kandel decided on a profession, as he writes in *In Search of Memory*, he chose psychiatry so that he could find where in the human brain the ego, the id, and the super ego resided. In his research, he discovered that that unholy triad did not exist in a locus but was a construct of mind. He saw that Freud was right—we are chemistry. Kandel took the notion to the extreme to show us how the mind sees, how the mind constructs reality, how the man exists in his moments of Forget. He showed us how art filters into a mind and how edges do not exist except as gradations of light and dark.

The princely mind is lost in a Paleolithic swamp of selfishness, never seeing or understanding who or what it is. It lives only in the first of the selective triads—wealth. Wealth to the princely mind buys position. Wealth buys power. But forgiveness? No sin, no crime, no transgression cannot be erased with wealth and so the princely mind is not accountable to anyone or anything. But the glorified Self it worships is a sham.

Thomas Gray writes—

The boast of heraldry, the pomp of pow'r,
And all that beauty, all that wealth e'er gave,
Awaits alike th' inevitable hour.
The paths of glory lead but to the grave.

The princely mind that lives in a constant denial of death also lives in a universe of ignorance and dies in a splurge of nothingness, because the arrogant prince does not see himself as human evolved from others who brought forward the container of life. He sees himself as a great and powerful being, *sui generis*, the self-made man who owes nothing to the rest of humanity. In this arrogance, he reaches the pinnacle of shame.

The arrogant prince lives in a darkness of mind where there is no light except the light that fires his own eyes.

The princely mind is an impoverished island devoid of compassion, empathy, sympathy, and unity. To be human is to understand how we came to be and how we share not just the same brain but the same constructs of mind. We are, each of us, the center of our universe and we all die alone, but the good among us go beyond the ego to feel the lives around us, to feel with each breath the anguish of being human.

I recently read *Sapiens: A Brief History of Humankind*, by Yuval Noah Harari. It is a book that acts as a summa. In it, Harari gives an overview of the history of human beings and asks the fundamental question: "What are we?"

Are we simply a mindless union of X and Y chromosomes led into the now so that we, too, can project the chromosomes into some unknowable future?

It is a good question. If we do not ask this question, then we all become arrogant in our treatment of life. We kill, we destroy, we annihilate, because we can, and in destruction, create our own earthly desert devoid of everything but us.

The princely mind, then, is a projection of a future replete with insanity, pain, terror, destruction, and the filth of unfettered ego.

In the words of a poet, we are more than flesh and bone.

Harari asks the question, "what is a human?" I ask the question, "is the arrogant prince even human?" Do wealth, position, and power define the future? Without victims, there are no strongmen. Strongmen depend on the weak for their wealth, their power, their position. Without the others, there is no pinnacle upon which the arrogant prince can stand. Is there anything left in the princely mind of the pain of ancestors? Is there anything left in the princely mind of the concept of the *commons*?

In this time, we have seen, as Garrett Hardin writes in *The Tragedy of the Commons*, how the range of the commons has been extended from that small patch of pasture that defined the original commons to the seas, and, in our time, to the space in which the Earth exists.

In short, the arrogant princes in their arrogant mania have despoiled the planet, and now they are in the process of despoiling the space around the planet. The princely mind has to be an extension of the biblical dictum, be fruitful and multiply.

This dictum is the life breath of an ever-expanding capitalism. Capitalism says we need more consumers to feed the coffers of the princes. So we must abhor abortion, we must control women's bodies, we must abhor birth control, because each baby is a mouth, a consumer, possessed of an infinite hunger for things, and that hunger feeds the arrogant princely mind its wealth. But it is our own greed and our own proliferation of Self that is the agent of destruction. If we say no, the princely mind will shrivel back into its meager slime and cease to exist.

The princely mind tells us that death is our due. On this path, there is no end but extinction. As the commons is depleted there is nothing but death. In the princely mind lies the end of humanity.

MAY 13

THE WISDOM OF PAIN

All we have is the body. We own things, we live in houses, we build families, but the body is all we have. When it is not whole, there is pain.

The body cannot be parted. It can be tattooed, but the tattoos are not the body but *on* the skin of the body. The tattoo can be erased, but the only erasure allowed the body is death.

When the body is whole, it works without conscious thought. The brain controls the body, but the mind does not measure the body at work.

When the body is not whole, the whole breaks down. And then we see the terror of not being intact. When we are intact, we are in balance. We walk, we move. Some of us move with grace and ease, while others amble, or trot, or move awkwardly. When we are whole, some of us do admirable and incredible things, while some of us are trapped in the darkness of pain and torture. When the whole is broken, we lapse into a helpless state of being that smells of death and defeat. The body is not meant to be partitioned.

The wisdom of being whole lies in the skin bound to flesh bound to bone. To be whole means to be intact and to move with the grace of an animal. We own things, but at the end, there is only the body, ground down by time.

When I read about death, when I think of the dead who are now not, there is a loose kind of envy as I see them free of worry and isolated from the skin, lying only in the bone and teeth.

Wisdom of the body means knowing what it is, who it is, and sometimes even knowing why it is there and how it got to be what it is.

The body disintegrates in time, but the horror of living a long life is to see the body fall apart, while the mind recalls what once was and never will be again.

The body, when whole, works so well that the muscles and the bone joined together breathe as one. And yet, when pieces of it break, the mind takes apart the whole. Gracefulness dies with the breaking apart and the ease of moving fades into pain and there is no good sleep when the body is not whole. I wanted to write about the skin of time and time eroding the skin just as rain erodes the mountain. The measure of loss is never bitter in the young, who do not see in their skin the grinding down—and maybe that is good, to let the young believe the body is eternal and complete and will always be what it is now.

But as it breaks, the body betrays the mind. Is there a wisdom of body? Does the body know what it needs? As I read into the new model of being, the answer suggested is no, the body does not know what it needs. The body does not say "I need more calcium" so it drinks more milk. The body does not say "I need more protein." The body will die without ever being aware. Ions in the blood force the body to devour its own bone, and in eating itself, the body breaks down and it dies.

The body does not "know." What the mind knows is the residue of experience. The body cannot predict what it will be, but at the same time, the mind can imagine not being. The body does have a wisdom but it is not wise. It is not a wisdom that can move between generations. It cannot know what it does not know, and in not knowing, it is always at the end of time.

I regret so many things. I regret that I will not know the end of any time except my own. I regret that my body will give out before I see my grandchildren grown. I regret that my mind will devour my being to the point of not being and then I will not know even the day or the hour or the year. Measuring time is our invention. The time of the body is not measured in seconds and minutes. The time of the body is measured in decay. To age is to lose—a piece at a time—that which made you proud and that which made you vigorous and beautiful and desirable. Desire itself might be a clock of the body.

In the new paradigm of being, others suggest that time does not exist at all, but that the spinning of an electron is from left to right or, in fact, is clockwise, which suggests a force of time and space. The body born as it is of electrons all moving in unison clockwise suggests a direction to time. I regret that I will not see the result of being, and it follows that I lament mortality.

I return often to Marcus Aurelius, whose *Meditations* speak to a mind through time. In his writing, I sense more connection than I have ever felt in the Bible or the Koran or the Bhagavad-Gita, because Marcus does not try to make something out of nothing. He writes that the only connection a mind, meaning a human, need worry about is the connection to the community. In his wisdom, Marcus writes long before it was known that we are a result of the being of others and do not need god or gods, because the only and last being of any importance is nature. The way he writes it, Marcus can put a capital N on nature because he knows that nobody can know that the eternal return is not to some abstract Valhalla or to some patriarchal and invisible heaven or to some terrible hell but to the dirt and the rock, to the sand and the flowers.

I regret that I will never be as wise as Marcus Aurelius. I know some of what he knew, but he knew more than I will ever know.

The body, the wisdom of being whole, is integral to this chain of being. I do know that when the body is no longer whole, this speed of being slows down and the movement that is used to define me now gets to the point of insight that lets John Verrall tell me he is mastering the art of sitting.

Two roads diverge in the distance, and I see to the left, the wisdom I will never have and to the right, the wisdom I wish I had. I come to a still point.

Enantiodromia.

The still point of opposites of equal power controlling all movement. I come to that still point boxed between the left and right. I come to the still point and stand in the agony of being.

What is wisdom?

How do you get it?

How do you know you have it?

How do you know that you don't have it?

I struggle with the body no longer being whole, its wholeness betrayed by time, and I struggle with my own ignorance. What do I know that can be of any use to another human being?

Is all wisdom personal, or is it, as my friend Robert Ray says, the distillation of time and space into a nugget of being. An aphorism—"No man is wiser than his time."

To be wise is to know what you don't know. To be wise is to know what not to say and when not to say it. Accepting these premises, silence can be mistaken for wisdom, but the listener does not know the strength it takes to remain silent.

MAY 17

THE WISDOM OF THE BODY

The wisdom of skin. The wisdom of bone.

The skin and bone you do not take with you. The skin remembered in its smoothness is a nostalgia for the time when you were young and beautiful and desirable before the time of your wounds.

The body wounded becomes conscious of its wound. Movement—the simple lifting of an arm becomes an exercise in pain. I sometimes imagine the sum of all the pain women have felt as they dealt with the men who seemed born to abuse them—burning them, stoning them, killing them, raping them. I imagine all that pain in one place and I know the Earth will throb with the excess and the fear. And I ask, why?

Does the body have its own wisdom of Self apart from Consciousness?

I have written about the body in sleep. I have felt myself awakening from deep sleep unaware in the depth of REM that my body, while I slept, had run through its play with time and filled my bladder without my awareness.

As I come back to consciousness, I return mind and brain to body and I have to evacuate my bladder—to take a leak. In its sleep, the body continues without me. I am in it, I am in the skin of the body, but the mind is not present while the brain works and the blood flows. It is this wisdom that I track now. What part of me dies in sleep? What remains of what I was yesterday? Does the daily wisdom die each night cycle to be reborn?

No.

Memory must remain in the body, silent and asleep, to return as the body awakens with its full bladder.

The wisdom of the body lies somewhere in the autonomic nervous system. I do not choose to breathe. I do not choose to have my blood flow. I do not tell the immune system to fight the toxins I ingest each day. I do not choose to have my kidneys fill my bladder with the dying elements of living. All of that is beyond mind. It is solely body and time.

There is a wisdom, a silent wisdom invested in the skin and bone, born in the blood in the brain that lies beyond knowing.

In living, there is so much I take for granted.

There is, then, the deeper wisdom of inherited being over which I have no control either, even no knowledge of as I lie in dead sleep. Awakening, I come into being again—being is not just an aware mind that centers on Self.

I understand, now, the wisdom of genes—it is not a thinking wisdom of mind and body, but an apartness that fuses the "I" and the "They," and out of all that fusion comes the "We."

The We. We are. In the wisdom of the body. I ask the question: What is sex?

Most sex is not procreative at all.

In the human passing of genes one to the other, only once in nine months is there procreation. Between that and birth, all sex is recreational. I ask myself when We, I, They made that connection and then made that leap.

I have written about the archaeology of toilets in England and France, where the cesspools reveal hundreds if not thousands of sheep-intestine condoms. French letters, the English called them. *Lettres anglaises*, the French call them. They had just one function—one purpose—to turn the corner from procreation to recreation in the discovery that sex is pleasure.

The mind knows that, but the body does not. The body's awareness of desire is embedded in the entwined strands of DNA. The body releases itself from its Self as it deals with desire—desire that is indifferent to purpose—not knowing (as it does not know) that the mind found a way around the mystery when it disconnected sex from procreation. Imagine, as I imagine, the pain of women amassed, our time in skins, in caves, in huts and stone. When did we make the leap across the barrier of desire and turn desire into joy?

I imagine a cave, I imagine a fire in a hearth and a man mounting a woman in the shadows, and the inevitable, ever happening exchange of sweat and semen and vaginal exudate—the chemistry of desire—and the momentary ceasing of mind in the small death. I ask myself, "what is the evolutionary adaptation to orgasm? Have women always orgasmed, as have men? Or, are we like beasts for whom desire is not in the mind at all, but buried in the body and bone alone?"

Sarah Hrdy writes that the female langur monkeys do not orgasm during or after sex. She writes that when the alpha male is replaced by a stronger male, a more fit alpha, the females in the troop abort their fetuses, the male kills the offspring of the vanquished alpha, and the females go into estrus and the new alpha mounts them serially. Planting his DNA as reward for his victory.

As I imagine the fire in the hearth in the shadow of sex, I see the primate in rapture without thinking. Desire is not thought. Desire is not will. Desire is a simple conceit—DNA must drive forward.

That is the foundation of being on this planet Earth. Everything else is a means.

The male is built for that and that alone, so what was the female in the cave thinking as she yielded? Was she thinking? Did she know what she was doing? Or did she simply do what desire drove her to do, driven by something in herself that she was not aware of?

Has thinking ever interrupted the passing of genes?

Before the Babylonians and the Egyptians wrote their treatises on pregnancy and abortion, what did they do? They wrote their treatises on contraception, but what brought us to that split between the fire in the hearth and the French letters in English latrines?

We know we have been tricked by desire, but why?

What is the burden of conception and why and how do the langurs—without drugs or coat hangers—abort the fetus of the beaten alpha?

Did we have that ability at one time?

If so, when did we lose it?

It seems that the couple with all its complexity and complexes must be the engine of destiny. A couple not living in the troop but living as two become living metaphors for the X and Y chromosomes, each separate from the other twenty-two chromosomes, the essential *sine qua non* of human existence.

When We and They made the separation, the tribe came into existence, but the strong male, the alpha, never willingly yielded in personal combat.

In the history of France, it is the mother's brother who is the link to the next generation. The son always knows who his mother is, but paternity is a clouded sky.

In France, the strongmen set up the law of the *droit de seigneur*—the right of the Lord of the Manor to have first sex with the newly wed bride.

In this way, the strongman pushed himself out into the future. It is now known that a certain percentage of the Western population descends from a limited number of males, and so the troop complex is not in abeyance here. But in the twenty-first century, at least in the West, it is not an issue.

It is said that a certain percentage of all the human beings in Mongolia are direct descendants of Genghis Khan. The Khan kept a harem. He copulated with his subject females. The troop had not passed by the thirteenth century.

The wisdom of the body prevails—the Khan was a strongman and he was a virile man and he was persistent.

The wisdom of the body, then, is not in the skin, but in the blood and the semen, and this we do know: Beta, Delta, and Gamma males do not leave legions of flesh bearing their mark.

In *Too Many Women*, the authors discuss the failure of the Y chromosome to pass, and that failure lies in the physical and social position of the males. Yes, males are a breeding experiment run by females, and females do not choose the lesser or the weaker.

Resources become more important than genes, and the wisdom of the body for a woman is of a different ilk than the wisdom is for the male.

The difference between female and male wisdom lets us see that rape and forced inseminations are violations of the natural law embedded in the body and desire.

There is no fire now, no hearth now, no shadow—but the choosing is clear. It is women who choose, and they choose because even if they do not "know" it, their choice is embedded in the body. Eggs are expensive, sperm are cheap, and that lays down the first tenet of natural law—the species hinges on choice by the female.

What she might choose, however, changes through time.

That woman in the cave, what was she choosing for?

THE WISDOM OF THE BODY, CONTINUED

Today, I'm writing more about the wisdom of the body.

Wisdom. I ask again the questions:

What is it?

How do you get it?

Why do you want it?

In *Trio of Lost Souls*, I wrote about Jim Garret's struggle with wisdom. As Jim Garret told us, wisdom isn't something you wait for.

If you don't know what it is, how do you know where to look and how do you know if you've found it?

Wisdom has this terminal reality to it. I think of the Greek concept of the firmament and how the Greek thinkers could not handle the retrograde motion of the planets and so invented the epicycles to explain why Mars seems to run backwards at certain times. When the terracentric model fell away, replaced by the heliocentric model, and the notion of orbital differentials took hold, we learned that Mars' seemingly backward movement is due to the variable speed of the orbits. As Earth passes

Mars, it leaves Mars behind, and the wisdom of three thousand years is useless. Obsolete. Redundant. Wisdom or knowledge?

Wisdom has some relation to knowledge and knowledge has some relation to experience as the *sine qua non* of science.

The experiment.

What I know of the body tells me that when the body is intact, it seems invisible, as if a mystical separation of mind from body has occurred. But the moment the body breaks—if any of it breaks—the break slams bone into reality. When the body is not intact, it becomes the focus of being.

As I take my vitamin B-complex tablet each morning, I ask myself, "do I need this? How do I know I need it?"

I tore my rotator cuff while exercising, and for six months, I could not write. In the past, when I wrote, I was not aware of the writing, not aware of the body as I wrote, but I was aware of the words.

Then, the Fall.

The shoulder is not just a muscle—it is a complex joint of muscles, tendons, blood vessels, desire. For a writer, the shoulder is an intricate part of the writing body, and once the body is broken, the words stop. It was not just the hand that writes—it is the body. The micro-movements of finger on pen require the movement of the entire shoulder and its muscles. I am diminished when bones break.

Pain is the reality of existence.

I cannot count pain, I cannot measure anguish, but I know that when the shoulder does not work, I am less than I was and the loss can be measured. As I write at this table for forty-five minutes, I know I will capture between twelve hundred and fifteen hundred words—words taken from the body via some mechanism that doesn't just defy logic but shreds it. There is no reason why I should be able to write, but I do. Two days a week, eight days a month, six months without writing means that I lost seventy-two thousand words. Words that I will never see written. Shoulder broken. Words lost. Words not captured from the flow of words living somewhere in me and being somehow accessible to the pen from which they flowed.

The body, then, has wisdom of pain and loss. I can measure the loss, just as Mitch in the novel, *Blood,* measured the sperm count of the prisoners around him. Three hundred million sperm lost in each ejaculation. Ten ejaculations a month, three billion sperm lost. And that was for just one prisoner.

Wisdom of loss is not only a measure of words or sperm, but a measure of the slow cutting away of the body with the time-scalpel. The loss is not measurable without clocks until the body breaks, and then the loss is real—I cannot run as fast as I once did. I cannot see as well as I once did. I cannot lift what I once lifted.

Loss is a cutting away that I measure only by looking backward at what once was.

In *The Fragile Wisdom*, which looks at the evolution of the body and its epigenetics, author Grazyna Jasienska asks, "does the body know what it needs? Can the body," she asks, "know that it needs meat or vitamin C? Does it know it needs salt or sugar?" She answers each question with "No."

The body does not know, but it does break if it does not get what it needs. Lose vitamin C, and the body loses teeth. Lose vitamin B, and the bones bend. Lose vitamin D, and the skin breaks out in a rash.

The body, she writes, knows nothing but the wisdom of others, and the wisdom of others has come down as knowledge through observation and experience, through doing and watching.

So the body is not wise in itself except, as Marcus Aurelius writes, within its community. In community we find the collective wisdom that tells us the value of gingko, of vitamin C, that shows us the truth of oranges and the value of sunshine.

It is the community, Marcus writes, to which you have a duty, and when you lose that knowledge, you become stupid and alone and you die.

American psychologist Harry Harlow and his monkeys taught us the truth of grooming. The monkey who is not groomed by the collective becomes aberrant and withdrawn. Without the community bond, the monkey descends into a state of apathy. What measures the monkey also measures the human primate.

In the Romanian orphanages, babies were stored in white rooms on white sheets with white lights, stored without the healing touch or the loving touch. In a predictable outcome of a stupid collective wisdom, they grew up untouched and broken. The mind had broken, just as bones break.

Without touch, the body dies. The mind warps, the emotions curdle.

The Romanian orphanages showed us what Harlow showed us—the primate is a touching beast. Without touch, we become shells. This is the collective wisdom garnered through observation and shown as knowledge—what to do.

My wife, Helen, did some language research in Mexico where she showed us the effects of the shawl culture. The Indian women bundled their babies against their bodies. They held them tight, they held them all day, but they did not speak to them much. Middle-class women did not bundle their babies. They held them in cribs and strollers and walkers, but they did talk to them.

The Indian babies were slow to develop language but they were happy. The middle-class babies cried much more but had early language.

Wisdom, then, is knowing what to do and when to do it to get a specific result.

Wisdom is also knowing what not to do—do not leave your babies alone, untouched, in white rooms on white sheets.

As I dig deeper into this, I keep coming up against silence.

Helen's work made it clear that early silence stymies a certain development.

What I am entering now is an era of quiet. I will call it the Time of Late Silence.

In the Time of Late Silence, I find a wisdom of the unsaid. Often what is said is not necessary and often it is not useful.

In French culture, the French seem not to mind silence while in American culture we find it abhorrent.

I see silence as a time to prepare to stop. To prepare for the shutting down. I know now the value of waiting in silence. Say what needs to be said. Speak only when it is necessary to keep the community bond intact.

We are hairless apes, and we stroke one another with words, we groom one another with accolades and promises.

This is the wisdom of silence.

In it, I finally see what I am doing and who I am and why.

But, now, I also ask the other question: "What do I do with silence?"

Can silence be the cement and the glue of community? I don't think so. We have moved away from our roots. We have substituted money for cabbage and bullets for stones. We have substituted being for wisdom.

As we move into the new world of genetic manipulation, we decay. We blunder into the new science as though we understood four billion years of evolution, but we do not. We are without the knowledge to proceed, although we know that in proceeding, we will make mistakes. Still, we persist.

I think we are not wise enough as a race to construct afresh what evolution has taken four billion years to accomplish.

MAY 24

THE WISDOM OF FORGETTING

The written word tends to be conservative. The spoken word seems to encourage change. Spoken Italian, French, Portuguese, Spanish are children of Vulgar Latin. The texts of the Roman writers, the written language, exists as the writers wrote it, but the spoken Latin evolved into regional dialects that in time became national languages. Speech is change.

In every language, there are two languages. The written word and the spoken word. Raymond Queneau's *Exercices de Style* is a stylistic tour de force. One hundred versions of a single event written in a hundred different styles, from hyperbolic to rhetorical.

In his novel, *Zazi dans le Métro*, Queneau opens with a single word in the spoken language—*Quesquipuedonktan*? which parses out in the written language as *Qu'est-ce qui pue donc tant*?

With this stylistic quirk, Queneau shows us that the spoken language is dynamic. He shows us that it changes. He shows us that, in fact, change is the essence of the spoken word. And in this snippet of dialogue, we see the confrontation between the learned and the not.

There is a modicum of wisdom in the spoken language and I want to explore that, but right now I want to get into the wisdom of forgetting. I know now less than I knew twenty-five years ago. Some of the wisdom of forgetting is to protect us from pain and the anguish of memory. There is, in forgetting, the question of the temporality of wisdom, the experience of knowledge, and the usefulness of facts.

At one time, I could quote dozens of poems in French—poems by Verlaine, by Rimbaud, by Villon, even Victor Hugo. I knew Garcia Lorca and had translated many of his poems. But now, all I can do is meditate on those forgotten words.

Here is one question that keeps coming back: What is the function of forgetting? Do we forget because what we know is obsolete, and knowing it, move on? Do we forget because our brain with its memory stores is wearing out? Is forgetting psychological, physical, neurological, or willful?

Mais où est le preux Charlemagne? But where is the valiant Charlemagne?

At one time I needed to know the origin of every word in that Villon poem to pass the PhD exam in philology.

I had to know every word in *Raoul de Cambrai*, its origin in Latin and the process that gave it its form in old French.

But now? Out of the past come only certain words and phrases—"*Carles li reis, nostre emperere magnes set anz tuz pleins ad estet en Espaigne.*" That is the opening of *La Chanson de Roland.* I know those words, but in their temporality as knowledge they lose their value. The fate of wisdom, it seems, is to lose its value through time. When I was an undergraduate, I took a course in astronomy. On the final exam, there was this question: "The surface of the moon is covered with a coat of dust how thick?"

The correct answer at that time was six feet (or two meters) of dust. Then, Neil Armstrong landed on the moon and the truth was known—the moon is covered with five-to-six inches, or ten centimeters, of dust. For years, I knew that the moon was covered in six feet of dust only to find out that it was not so—so the answer on my final exam that was right then is wrong now.

The temporality of wisdom leads to the temporal nexus of wisdom. What else of what I know contains its six-feet-of-dust problem?

I don't know.

But I do know that as I age I forget, because much of what I know is no longer of any value to me and certainly of no value to any other human being.

I meet people every day who do not need to know the answers to all the philological questions that I solved on my PhD philology exam.

At the writing table today, someone read the start line, "She crumpled her napkin." In six hours I will have forgotten that sentence. Then, when I dictate this writing, it will come back, but only because it is written down.

The protective shield of Forget is very thick. So thick that sometimes what I used to know cannot penetrate into the now.

I wake up each morning with a stanza of a song in my head. Never the whole song, just a few lines, a verse or two that I repeat. For two or three hours, I hear that song. I sing the words. But then, somewhere in time, it vanishes and I can't remember any of it. I can remember that I was singing it, but it is gone and I know this—it will never come back. I cannot will it into being. I cannot force myself to recall the song I sang yesterday. Each morning, there is a different song. It is as if in singing, I empty the vault holding the song and banish it forever from memory.

This, I know: The retrieval of information plays on the information and what goes back into memory is changed such that were I to recall it again, the replaced fact becomes a new fact sometimes not related at all to the original.

The criminologist tells us that this is the problem with eyewitnesses—the brain creates a reality so that memories are not what we think they are. What we recall today is not what we recalled yesterday. Facts are not what we recall them being.

I float on a sea of Forget. Forgetting, some neurologists tell us, is selective. You forget that which you do not need to recall. You forget to recall that which will harm you.

Once, years ago, when talking to my friend Bruce Saunders, I told him that I'd had an epiphany. It was as if my brain had opened up and released everything I knew. I felt knowledge disappearing. I watched years of reading slip into a fog, and the fog become nothing. Now the question is, where does Forget go? Where does the forgotten go? What is the purpose of forgetting? If you forget facts, what have you forgotten? Where are all the facts of yesteryear if they are no longer in my brain?

Mind, the neurologist tells us, is what brain does. Brain needs to create a narrative in order to explain its existence. But what is the narrative without facts? Where are my facts now? Where are all the things I knew when I answered the questions on the French PhD exams?

As I read—and I read every night, neuroscience, history of science, anthropology, novels, stories—if I am "lucky," I remember perhaps one item of what I have read, but there is no guarantee I will recall it or that I will ever use it.

Last week, I discovered several science magazines I know I read when they came out. As I read them again, the facts in them were released from their temporality—the Neanderthals had language. They had art. We killed them off. But later, I read in another magazine that we share as Homo sapiens a certain percentage of Neanderthal DNA. Anthropological research now tells us that we did not kill them off; we slept with them until we had absorbed them.

Facts are the foundation of knowledge. Knowledge is the foundation of wisdom. Wisdom is the measure of my meaning so that when my facts disappear, part of my meaning disappears as well.

I am what I can pass on. I am nothing if I know no facts. My facts slid away. As I read those magazines, I was discovering facts that were years-old and obsolete. Those facts were written down. And this bothers me. I need to know that I am more than flesh and bone. As I wrote in "The Painted Interior," I need to know that there is something beyond meat. Why? Why is that a question? My unique arrangement of facts that I meld into my wisdom makes me who and what I am. If speech changes through time and facts are encoded in speech, then must the details of the facts evolve, too?

In my novel, *Doubles in a Game of Chance*, the protagonist, Dalton, makes this discovery: "Because all meetings were secret and eyes only, many of the policies which RCC dictated came down without any written record and so much of what seemed to be policy was simply faulty recollection."

There is a deep and awful agony in Forget. What you once recalled with ease is now impossible to retrieve. And there is nothing you can do about it.

Facts released from time vanish, and there is no retrieving them. Reading something again is no guarantee that its facts will return. In the depths of his catatonia, where he sat for days, the composer Robert Schumann would emerge from time to time to say, "I have these terrible recurring fits of sanity."

In Forget, there is release from pain and present, release from future and past. But until complete darkness takes your mind, you have these horrible, recurring fits of sanity in which you realize that what you once knew no longer exists within you. You remember the forgetting but never the forgotten.

The pain is in knowing that you can never be again what you once were.

I spent a year exploring my mind with Rose Katz, a Jungian psychologist who specialized in working with artists. She told me that I needed a new set of tools to get me through the last third of my life. After talking to Rose, after investigating my inner secrets and the things that lay hidden in my mind, I was able to break free from the process of writing the same story over and over again. In talking to Rose, I sat down and began a new system of writing. I was able to write the novel *Blood*, followed by the novel, *Gabriela and The Widow*. In these novels, I found a new direction for my writing. Leaving behind the old, forgetting everything that I had known before, I set out on a new track. Or was it new? Was the "new" way a simple reorganization of the residue of the old still inhabiting my mind? Looking at the new work, I see the ashes of the old. The words are common, the sentences still have a subject and an object, sometimes. The connection between words still exists so that the writing is not a word salad. In the new, I am looking at the residue of a lost world of the mind, a world I do not remember creating. It stands in the writing as though it has been there forever, when in fact, it only came into being a short while before.

This is the wisdom of forgetting. It allows you to leave who and what you were behind and launch yourself again into a future that only you can shape.

THE TEETH ALWAYS REMAIN

It is now a year since I started to write these essays.

In a year, I have broken my body in many ways.

I have gained a few insights and lost many facts.

Still, I write.

I no longer know what I used to know, and in some way, I am diminished as a man, as a person, as a writer.

Today, I write about teeth in the broken body.

When there is nothing left of our flesh, the teeth remain.

The teeth always remain.

Three million years after the flesh has decayed, the teeth mark where each of us last lay.

We have died on the prairies, we have expired on the savanna, and we have disappeared from the mountains, but always the teeth remain.

In time, there is little that lasts, but the teeth, the stones in the mouth, leave a legacy of our passing. The stones in the mouth tell the story. From the stones in the mouth, you can see what, as children, we ate. You can see the residue of the water we drank on our journey.

Some of us chewed grasses that left striations on the stones in the mouth, and from those striations we can read the age, the place, sometimes even the heritage left in the ancient DNA. In our passage through time, the small double helix dissolves and its dissolution masks the mystery of who we are.

Even now, who we are is buried in Deep Time. Few of us ever travel past the great grandfather. Deep Time swallows who we were—takes the name, takes the body, but leaves the teeth.

The white stones in the mouth anchored to the bones of the jaw—and of that, there is only a mystery. Who was here? Did she have a name? When did we begin to name the body? When did we begin to say the words?

The mouth and the teeth are in place, tightened by muscles that give shape to sound. Before the shaping, there were teeth, but before the shaping, there were no words.

Can we imagine those feet walking through the sand, crossing over the stones, fording the river before the shaping gave us sound?

As I read Eric Lenneberg's *Biological Foundations of Language*, I see who and what we are in the muscles. I see what we were in the placement of the hyoid bone. I know that before the muscles shaped our sound against the teeth, we hooted and screeched but we did not name. The naming came late in the journey, along with tools and ideas, and with ideas and tools came culture and the telling.

Without the muscles and the bone and the stones in the mouth, there was no telling, and we died in Deep Time. In the teeth, there is a wisdom of time, because in the residue of time that encrusts the ancient teeth, we read not just the eating of the grass in the silica striations, but we also read the lineage before Forget. To forget means to see the *now* severed from time. But first there had to be something to remember. Here, in the mouth, in the stones in the mouth is the trail of Forget.

Who were we before we spoke?

What did we teach the young before the shaping?

I look back in time, into Deep Time, and in that time, I see us walking. "Step here, do not step there." The first words taught us that there are traps and how to avoid the traps, and if you do not avoid them, you die.

How do you tell the young to "step here" if there is no shaping of the sound against the teeth? In the teeth and in the bone, in the muscles of the face, the shaping comes together and with it, comes the telling. Without the telling, we are not. Without the telling, we are only teeth left in the dirt of time. The telling endured only after we first made scratches in mud, marks in the dirt, when we first read the animal tracks and someone named the animal and someone wrote the sound that before had lived only in the mouth but now lives forever in the writing, even with Forget.

Teeth are our residue. The teeth mark where we were but do not mark where we are going—there is so much mystery to being. So much unknown about the passing, but from the teeth, in the teeth, we see what we ate. Our bacteria leave their own residue in us on the stones in the mouth. We read that residue now, and in reading it, we see what we once were.

What we are now will someday be three million years ago, and in that "ago," there will be a record—in the teeth.

What puzzles me now is how we got so stupid. The trajectory we were on did not project our stupidity. We see in the residual evolutionary responses how we once were, and we see how what we were shapes what we are.

In time, the stone became the bullet, the bullet became the bomb, and, as if our sole purpose were not to survive but to kill, now becomes clear in the residual evolutionary responses to baby fat, to body, to size and shape.

How did that happen?

All we were came together, leaving only us. Only us, the word-users.

From bacteria, we came to be, and in being we became more, until now we live side-by-side in such numbers that we step to the edge of extinction.

Maybe this is what our teeth tell us: Because we are too many, we choose to cease to be.

Is that possible?

A collective will to die?

In the killing, we see the residual evolutionary response to living worked out in death.

We have become so good at killing, and as we become better, we will see nothing left to kill except ourselves. So we perfect the killing of ourselves as though we have another biological imperative driving us to extinction. And the art? Without the art, we are nothing but a tribe of expert killers.

We must kill, and we do kill, and when there are no more animals to kill, we will kill each other until there are too few of us, and those few will die their own kind of death, a death too horrible even to imagine.

Maybe this is what the teeth buried three million years tell us. The long arc of our narrative has a beginning in stone, and as the stone took flight and we learned to kill at a distance, maybe, then, our destruction was set. As we play it out in death and in the revealed texts of single men speaking for all of us, we see our end.

But the stones in the mouth will remain. They have remained even when the bacteria ate the rest of us. The teeth tell our story, tell us about the shaping of sound that names objects, and in the naming, sets a long arc of our story. The teeth remain.

After three million years, they remain.

And this simple fact astounds me so much—to think that of all we have been, only the teeth remain as evidence of who we were.

Sometimes in the dark, as I lie half asleep, I run my tongue over my teeth and I imagine the time after the killing, after the slaughter that is coming, and I ask, "will there be enough of us left to pick up the teeth and wonder?"

There is coming a time after the shaping of sound when the only sound will be the moans and groans of the dying. In that dark time, there will be no return to a pure state, there will be no elevation to another space or time or spirit. The long arc of our journey will end and we will witness the first of the end now—there is so much killing among us. We, the sole survivors of the teeth-shaping sound, will disappear.

There are so many residual evolutionary responses driving us that there will be no more until we are no more. Then, as we disappear in time, only the teeth will remain.

As I read Montaigne's essays, I saw how easy it was to shift from light to dark, from wonder to worry. That is the way our minds work. That is the way the body has shaped our sound. I recall Montaigne's essay, "*Des Coches*" ("Of Coaches"), in which one would think he'd write about wheels. No, he writes about everything but wheels. He writes about pessimism and death and destruction and opulence.

There is more yet to be written about pessimism and death and modern greed and opulence, just as there is more to say about the stones and the teeth of the word-ape.

JUNE 2

WISDOM AND SILENCE, WISDOM AND NOISE

Silence is the endpoint of wisdom. Not the absolute silence of death, but the studied silence that comes only when you have learned the value of silence. Silence and noise, the ugly duo of our time, space, and culture. Noise disrupts the even flow of time, bequeathing nervousness, edginess, and tension that bloom into hatred—hatred of self, hatred of others, pure hatred.

As I write, I immerse myself in silence. I spend much of each day alone. In the solitude, I find not just peace, but a deeper desire for more silence.

Knowing when not to speak, as well as knowing the exact moment when to speak, spells wisdom. I have not yet reached that point. The lesson of the past few years has been an understanding of the selfie—the photographic selfie from the handheld cell-phone camera, the selfie of the "I" in all of its settings. Eating. Bathing. Sex. And there is the verbal selfie, the cry of anguish living in each of us in this age of anxiety and fear.

At the center of the verbal selfie is the personal memoir. And there is the other kind of selfie, the novel of the thinly disguised autobiography.

My lesson has been how to turn away from the "I"—not to dissolve it, not to demean the "I" of the other, but to keep from the self the self—best summed up in the clause, "I have been there."

This turning of interaction into the world of the "I" is the antithesis of the wisdom of silence.

To be silent does not negate opinion or knowledge, but it does measure the width of wisdom through time, when the "I" realizes the insignificance of self-aggrandizement. I ask myself as I listen to "the other" speak, will my experience enhance, enrich, add to, or detract from the now? Usually I come away with a "no."

"No" is the biggest word of all. Knowing when the negative has more force than the positive. Knowing when to say nothing, which is also a way to say no, is the most fruitful limb of wisdom.

In the early essays, I wrote about wisdom as knowledge and how knowledge is transient in a scientific universe. Today, I write about the silence of wisdom that does not share the knowledge but lays it quietly aside. Troublesome as it is, the rise of fervid religiosity in our time makes me impatient with the religious systems of belief polluting the world. To abide by my own wisdom and say nothing would be a betrayal, because to my way of thinking, religion is a failure of mind, of knowledge, a failure for being unable to accept the *divine silence* of the *deus absconditus* as an index to the truth of being.

In *Citadel*, Kaavi tells Trisha that there will be no peace until religion is banned forever from all the citadels.

In Constitution Hall in Versailles, a plaque celebrates the abolition of royalty. Only the French, with their abject devotion to Catholicism, would dare to take that step. In royalty is inherent the divine right of kings, and in the divine right of kings lies the *droit de seigneur*, which entitles the *seigneur* to the virginity of every woman in his domain. To deny royalty is to release women from sexual slavery, and in that, there is not just the future, but a truth for all time.

As Diderot wrote, "Man will never be free until the last king is strangled with the entrails of the last priest." Freedom can come only on a river of blood. Mao Zedong writes that a revolution is not a dinner party, that political power comes from the barrel of a gun.

So, I ask myself, what if these men had remained silent? To remain silent in the face of fascism is a crime even more egregious than fascism itself. So, in my desire for wisdom and its need to silence the Self, I am guilty of denial. In this denial, there is a collective shame. Shame rides our shoulders every day when we wake and see fascism rising and choose to do nothing—doing nothing, a form of silence. But what is to be done and where is it to be done?

Where is the barrel of the gun of political power in this time when the agents of law are themselves lawless murderers? Who does the good man kill, if kill he must, to arrive at a just and peaceful state? In a time of violence, is killing ever good? All of *Citadel* is built on the idea of the innate, inborn, inherited will to kill that unifies all of the evolved males of the modern state. The will to kill. What does that mean? It can mean that ideas are the fodder of death and belief gives license to kill. Are we in a transcendent state—not a precursor to enlightenment, but a state of interminable killing?

In his song "The Future," Leonard Cohen wrote "I have seen the future, brother, and it's murder."

Anarchy arrives on the back of murder. In Manila, the extra-judicial killings have no consequences for the killers. We are in a state of complete chaos when there are no laws to constrain, and constraint is the hallmark of civilization. Without constraint, there is no accountability, and the murderer goes free.

This is a time not for silence, but for speaking, even shouting—but with this caveat: If the ones we shout about are the killers, what is the recourse? There is none but that barrel of the political gun, and with that we devolve into civil war. No country ever recovers from its civil war or from a fascist state in which murder is legalized by the hands of the solons. To Jean-Jacques Rousseau, who wrote *Du contrat social*, the lawgiver was second only to God, because it is the solon who prescribes the laws by which humans govern themselves. But we have seen that in our time, the solons themselves do not condemn murder. We are now in a normal state of living with murder. It is to be our future, too.

Wisdom. Silence. Murder. The wise person cannot be silent in this time of chaos and death. Ernest Becker, in *The Denial of Death*, writes about how humans in America cannot accept death, and, so, we hide it. Death-denial increases with the geometric increase in population. In the increase, we see the lessening of value of a single life and so tolerate the killing. This is our shame and our guilt. There are sixty-four million Americans who appear to be arming themselves against some phantom threat, but in reality, they are the pawns of a segment of rich men who cannot tolerate a democratic society in which people they deem to be inferior actually pass laws that might impinge upon their goal of accreting wealth. These warriors—yes, warriors of the religio-capitalist caste—are indifferent to the terror they have created. In fact, they support the death state and its perpetrators and assassins. Where is the moral outrage when all constraint has been abolished?

In his novel, *Gargantua*, Rabelais writes of the Abbaye de Thélème, with its portal and its motto, *Fais ce que tu voudras sera le tout de la loi*. Do what you will shall be the whole of the law. We are there now, living in anarchy, living in death, daily, living in a time of blood and murder and indifference to it. In *Citadel*, Daiva writes through the character Kirsis that there are so many of us that maybe the Y chromosome, aware of its own decay, speaks to the mind of men and pushes them into a collective and cultural suicide. It is a bleak thought; it is a necessary one. How, in this time of such great achievements, in this time of such great scientific advances, in this time of times never seen before, is it possible for men to murder, to rape, to violate, to imprison others as if it were natural?

How, in the age of the cell phone, which gives the user access to a universe impossible even fifty years ago—how is state-sponsored murder possible?

Chaos. We, now in the Anthropocene, are reaping the rewards of our hatred of life. It seems that death must stalk us, as if we can no longer tolerate living.

Silence. As I write these words, I listen to a recording of *Perseverance,* the Mars lander, as it moves across the Martian landscape. Are the minds that created this robot and placed it on Mars the same minds that espouse and adore the *deus absconditus*? If the answer is yes, then I have to ask: "How have we persisted and thrived with such contradictions?"

JUNE 9

THE WISDOM OF FINISHING

To finish. To end. To bring to a stop. *Finis.*

The wisdom of finishing tells you that to finish is to understand how to begin. When I taught at conferences, I opened with this joke: Writers have just three problems—

How to start.

How to keep going.

How to finish.

When you lick those three, you are in.

The beginning predicts an end. The end is predicated on a beginning. For the writer, the worst thing that can happen is the full stop. A poem, I tell poets, should end, it mustn't just stop.

The idea of an ending implies a structure. The idea of structure implies a shape. A poem that stops has no shape. It has no ending. The wisdom of finishing creates its own problems.

How do you know when it's finished?

How do you know when to let it go?

If you stop instead of finishing, you have done nothing. Stopping is a bridge to nowhere, a road that dead-ends in the middle of the desert. A path to the top of nowhere.

Finishing, to me, implies a process: How do you begin in such a way that the ending is implied in the beginning? The wisdom of time gives us triplets. What walks on four legs in the morning, two legs at noon, three legs at dusk? The Sophoclean riddle implies a three-part structure. A life is divided into a beginning, a middle, and an end. We are born, we learn, we die.

The tripartite structure pervades the Western mind. In the wisdom of beginnings, we see the wisdom of finishing. But the sense of time in the West is broken. The question of time inserts itself into the question of the beginning.

Had I written in the time of the Maya, I might have seen time in units of katuns. I might have seen a cluster of katuns as a baktun. I might have seen a cluster of baktuns as a sun. I might have seen the fifth sun as the end of time. In the Maya mind, was the beginning inherent in the ending?

To the Maya, time cycles into a series of beginnings. But the continuum is a hard nut for the Western mind to crack.

Say that a life is on a continuum that can last for one day, one hour, one hundred years. Faced with that, how does the writer of memoir begin even to think of finishing?

I know this—to finish brings me a sense of joy. If I begin a piece, I start with emotion, feeling, or a sense of place. Then, I imagine an ending. Without the ending, I have no sense of direction, no sense of purpose, only a sense of going nowhere. To see an ending is to suggest a hundred beginnings, a hundred forks, a thousand choices. *If—then*, becomes the guide. If I do *this*, then my characters must do *that*. *If—then* is a chain of guideposts, of mile-markers along the way. If I have an ending in mind, then I can move from place to place on a line of divagations—subplots off the main line but always aimed at the ending, which might not be the ending you see at the beginning.

Implicit in this process is change and the idea of obstacle. No story moves in a straight line, except a dreadfully boring one.

The difference between a Johann Sebastian Bach fugue and a Max Reger fugue is the difference between a chance encounter with a beast in the jungle and an encounter with a beast in a cage in a zoo. The confinement of Reger limits the possibility of the fugue, whereas J.S. Bach, by introducing anomalies, produces a circus of accidents.

In nature, they say, there are no straight lines—except the lines in quartz crystals. Writing the straight line is the death knell for the writer. To finish is to integrate the accident, to see the obstacle as opportunity, to value the anomaly.

In the beginning is the unknown. The unknown we learn of as we go, and the logic of going implies that the end will be there. If I climb a mountain, I expect to arrive at a summit. From the summit, I see where I have been. I learned that Blake Edwards, who brought us the Pink Panther movies, started with an ending. He then said, "how did I get here? What comes before?"

So the wisdom of finishing suggests that the beginning can be found. In this idea, I develop the notion of the walk back through time. It works this way: You have a beginning. A moment in time. You ask yourself what happened five minutes, one hour, one week, one month, one year, four years before the opening.

This implies that the logic of the ending is that every beginning is already an ending. The complexity of structure exaggerates our consciousness and implies the work of the mind we cannot know. You cannot interrogate your unconscious mind using the apparatus of your consciousness. Consciousness is a narrow window, while the unconscious is a vast and complicated sea. It speaks only in metaphor, never in logical syntax, always in symbols, never in concrete objects with a single meaning. So the structure comes not from the conscious mind, but from the unconscious, as it tries to make sense of the journey.

Every story is a journey begging to be concluded. In this, as Aristotle says, art is an imitation of life. Life, however, is a defiant and rebellious child we spend years trying to tame, only to find that in taming it, we open other domains.

Finishing is, of course, a dream. If the beginning is an already-made ending, then there is no such thing as a finish, only another opening. Still, I can sense when a piece *feels finished.* I look at it, I see the way it develops, I see the plot points, and in the subplots, I watch characters develop with their objects, and I see the characters wrapping up their subplots aiming at the finale. When that happens, I, along with Conrad Aiken, say "*Tetelestai*"—it is finished. It is enough. Never the life, but this journey, and there can be hundreds of journeys in a life. To end is a problem. To begin is a problem. But never to end is a horror.

The wisdom of finishing, then, is to know how and why and what. How do you know? When is the beginning *the beginning*? When is the ending *the ending*? Do you know why an action happens and why the character reacts? In making these choices, we see both Pavlov and ourselves as creators. We make the character react; we build the world the character inhabits. And then what?

Always the existential questions: "What are we? What are we doing? Where are we going? What will we do when we get there?" In the beginning, the ending shows.

In the evolution of the mind—and mind is what the brain does—the ride-along questions are always: "Who are we? Is this real? Is this a dream?" I think of Pedro Calderón de la Barca and his *La vida es sueño*. Segismundo wakes up . . . or does he? Is he dreaming that he has just woken up? Is he dreaming that he is waking up in a dream that he is dreaming about waking up in? The mind is a labyrinth.

To finish is to accept nothingness, the answer to all these fundamental questions.

In the end, the writer has to ask, "is it done?" The answer is a cosmic silence.

JUNE 13

WISDOM AND WRITING

I read some of Mao Zedong's sayings in the *Little Red Book* today to find out the depth and wisdom of his thinking. Here is a man who changed human history. Not just in China and the East, but the entire political, social, industrial, intellectual, and agricultural fabric of the world.

I read the English translations, as I know nothing about Chinese. The sayings in translation are compressed, all the extras squeezed out, so I have to assume that in Chinese we see precision and compression. This gets us to the essence of good writing—economy.

It is clear that Mao knows what he wants to say, and he says it with the sharpest, most precise language. There is little bloat, and you see this if you look at several translations. The way Mao builds his aphorisms using successive clauses to increase the intensity and to hold off the conclusion gives us the correct way to handle subplot and character arc. Mao shows us that the good writer does not bury the lede or waste words but builds tension that leads to a climax. I'm surprised at how many of Mao's sayings are short lists of traits, and how many are logical extensions of a string of metaphors. Some of the sayings are single-verb, single-subject declarative statements, for example, "Women hold up half the sky." These are the tight aphorisms, some of which are buried in longer sections, but these are the aphorisms that some readers of Mao take as all of Mao. But the *Little Red Book* contains much about fear and death, conflict and resolution, struggle and defeat, community and capitalism. I was also surprised at how often Mao references American Blacks as an oppressed class under capitalism, oppressed by the reactionary elites, whose sole purpose is to turn labor into capital. I was impressed with how much of Mao's writing has the characteristics of fiction—conflict/resolution. Beginning, middle, end. Plot tracks, spine—in the sense of a string of metaphors that are all transforms of a central idea.

In reading Mao Zedong, I come to understand the force of language, not just as a tool for persuasion, say, of rhetoric, but as a tool for teaching. I understand that much of the *Little Red Book* was aimed at people who did not read and had no education but learned by listening. In this design, we can see the state of China just emerging from a condition in much the same way Western culture emerged as illiterate with the Bible and all of its visual representation indexing a cultural norm.

When Helen and I visited France a few years ago, we toured cathedrals to see the exegesis of biblical lore written in stone. The gist of this method is the following: In medieval France, people listened to the priest who told stories from the Bible that were carved into the friezes and the portals of cathedrals so the story was in fact written in stone—not as word, but as emblem. In this medieval art, I see the power of Mao, and I understand how the cult of the leader becomes both a political and a religious exercise. Can you then say that the *Little Red Book* has the power of a text for revealed religion?

I think so. What I see in this slim volume is how the elite seduced the proletariat into a certain state of mind that resulted, as all religious thinking does, in a limited view of the world and of the Other. I see art as liberation. I see film as revolution. I see the novel as the great tool for expanding the mind, because the mind—be it of a Chinese pre-Maoist peasant, a medieval French peasant, or a post-Mohammedan Arab—decodes all input using the innate apparatus of the mind. That apparatus is conditioned by the external source, the work of other men, other minds: Bible, Koran, *Little Red Book*. I turn to the basis of my own education—the French Enlightenment, where text did not come from revelation, but from investigation.

Today, as I was reading Mao, I recalled Denis Diderot, the Enlightenment encyclopedist and avid revolutionary, and I wanted to expand on his view of freedom. I would amend Diderot this way: There will be no freedom until the last lawyer strangles the last politician with the entrails of the last priest, then slits his own throat. Mao to the extreme.

The fate of women is anemic in all of these writings, because we had not yet accepted that women—Chinese peasants, medieval nuns, and French maids, as well as Irish maids and black American servants—are people. As I read the writings of Germaine Greer, Germaine de Stael, and as I read the writings of Betty Friedan and Helen Remick, I come to see that inherent in the writings of some of the philosophers, there was acknowledgment that women were humans. It is curious to me that the revealed religions do not admit that humanity but see women as property.

Mao writes that women hold up half the sky, but practice shows that women after the revolution were not accepted as the equals Mao suggests them to be. In post-Maoist China, women are still tools for procreation and the generation of capital.

Female babies are not desirable. Only boys count.

Today, as I returned to my book of essays on wisdom, I thought I would begin a reading of them to see what I had done. I came to an essay called "The Arrogance of the Princely Mind," in which I write that in the mind of the self-appointed elites in American politics, women are discounted. I write that women are complicit in their own subjugation when they accept the precepts of late-twentieth-century evolutionary trait selection.

In the Paleolithic past, women selected males for speed, size, and aggressiveness, whereas in our time, women select for wealth, power, and position. In 2016, as enslaved as ever, fifty-three percent of white women voted for a man who reduces women not of his class to body parts. In *Citadel*, Trish discovers that before the Separation in the East, women were given the number seven. Seven? Yes. In the East, women were seen as the sum of the holes in their bodies, plus their nipples.

As I read the *Little Red Book*, I see an ideal at work. I see the truth in Mao's capitalist critique that suggests each child is a mouth to feed, a body to clothe, a man to house, a woman to transport. All of this is predicated on two principles: oppose education, oppose birth control. The text is its pretext and its context: Women are not equal to men, for women are baby-producing consumers for the princely mind to increase his wealth, his position, and his power.

One of the artifacts of twenty-first-century trait selection is unimpeded access to many women. Women who might have rebelled at being slaves to the alpha male for whom speed, size, and aggression were dominant now fall prey to wealth—a sociological residual evolutionary response—not seeing in their choice the root of their own enslavement. In this preference, males who are not wealthy, powerful, or well-positioned come up short, their procreation limited. The princely mind, poisoned by religious precepts as useless as a rhinoceros horn, hoards women and produces children in vast quantities. At last count, No. 45—let him be known by his number as (the former) president of the United States—has seven offspring in an already obscenely overpopulated world.

I think Mao understood the problem, but Mao could not rewrite the human genome. So far, no one can do that, not even Doudna and Charpentier. Until we find a noninterventionist way to redraw human nature, we will continue to fuck ourselves into oblivion, driven by the precepts of revealed religion in its collusion with pernicious capitalism.

Eight billion mammalian weeds now thrive on the planet and more are coming.

We are victims of our own selective success.

And there does not seem to be a solution.

The human appetite for sex in the service of capitalism produces one horrific world, as billions of us shit and piss into the river, eat all the animals of the field, steal all the resources from any future idyllic world, and kill one another at an unprecedented rate.

THE WISDOM OF LIMITS

I started these essays with a portmanteau word—*irredundant*. Irredundant is a union of redundant and irrelevant. Since then I have done nothing original and that is my concern. Is there a limit to wisdom?

How can I begin to answer that question if I don't know what wisdom is? And so begins my list of repetitions:

What is wisdom?
How do we get it?
What do we do with it when we get it?
How do we know we don't have it?

I see some relationship between wisdom and knowledge. I see some connection between science and wisdom. I see some link between science and knowledge and wisdom. But I see no link between religion and wisdom.

My father was a brilliant man who held several patents. He knew how to build equipment that men used to tunnel underground. They used his equipment to keep themselves safe and alive. But when I visited my father in Mexico, just as he was at his peak of productivity and insights, I asked him why he didn't write a book containing everything he knew. His reply was informative: "When I die," he said, "I'll take it all to the grave with me."

I did not think of my father as a wise man, but later I saw the truth of his wisdom. In the time between his creative life and the time he died, his world changed. His was a world in which men drove tunnels with dynamite. They drilled the rock, they shot the rock, they hauled the rock out of the tunnel and took it to a spillway—the talus.

Just after I graduated from Berkeley, I was in New Mexico working on a Robbins mole with my father. I learned that the old way was giving way to the new. We did not drill and shoot. Using the mole, we bored a hole through the rock. Instead of hauling the shot rock to the talus, we used conveyor belts to move the detritus from the tunnel face to the trains and then to the outside. My father, as if by clairvoyance, knew the future of tunneling and the future of tunneling did not entail the use of dynamite.

Years later, in New Zealand, he ran a project with four moles and not one stick of dynamite, not one drill. His world had changed and everything he might have written in his book had already become obsolete.

Understanding my father leads me to see the relationship between science and wisdom. As the engineers and material scientists develop new methods and new metals, the whole idea of tunneling changes. My father, wise in the old ways, knew what to do, when to do it, and how to do it. This knowledge made him employable. But as the scientists learned more, my father's wisdom ceased to have meaning. Does wisdom decay in the mind as science bypasses it?

In trying to answer that question, I see now that wisdom, the way I have been thinking and writing about it, might be in and of itself obsolete in the new technology.

Once knowledge stopped being the sole domain of the priestly class, the world changed. We could call it democracy. In the past, writing was done largely by a few. The Sumerians, who wrote on clay, taught scribes to write using cuneiform script, the script that became the standard until CE 300, when it gave way to Greek and Roman writing.

The knowledge and wisdom of cuneiform died, until it was resurrected in translation years later, when it became known that the priests of Babylon not only knew about the orbits of Venus and Mars, but had developed a rudimentary theorem of calculus three thousand years before Leibniz and Newton. Babylonian wisdom lay concealed in cuneiform. So what is the longevity of wisdom? Does wisdom die, as my father suggested, when he said he would take it to the grave? Where does wisdom go to die? Is there a residue of wisdom still in the mind when people no longer know that there was a wisdom before them? The transience of wisdom is bothersome to me for its temporality. Time is not the keeper of knowledge, although time seems to move us in a direction. What we once held as solid, tangible wisdom that let us understand the world, fades.

My father's wisdom died but was replaced by another science. It is a science contained not in the mind of a single man, but in the collective, which is the science of the world. So, I have to ask, are the engineers wise? Do they have wisdom or do they just understand the mechanics of the world in this moment?

One of the characteristics of the ancient wisdom is that it was held only by a few—a few scribes, a few priests, a few bureaucrats. Today the democratization of knowledge seems to be flowing back to the way it used to be. A few coders understand the binary universe. Only a few scribes can read the new code. Only a few engineers can read the code and then turn the code into a machine. The servo-mechanism is the object in the physical world ignited by the binary code that is unreadable to the man on the user end of the machine. The wisdom of our time reverts to a few who know the *what*, the *when*, the *how* of the codable world.

The demise of the Enlightenment that began with Ronald Reagan lies in the secret binary codes. We see it everywhere when the computer fails. We are at a loss. The computer can be on your desk, in your lap, in your car, but when it fails, you are lost. You do not know how to fix it. You must take it to a priest of the binary code who reads the connection between the digital and the mechanical worlds. The priest of this darkness keeps the code from us and distances us from the secrets of the universe. This is not wisdom, is it? If wisdom is knowing what to do, how to do it, and when to do it, then yes, it is a wisdom but a wisdom that again devolves back to the elites, to the priests, to the keepers of secrets. So, wisdom is temporal and it is restricted.

Wisdom is compartmentalized and it becomes more so each day.

It is said that you don't need to know how a car works, you only need to know how to start it. True. But the moment the computer on your car fails, you are helpless.

It is written by the military historians that the Allies won World War II because many of the GIs were farm boys who knew how to fix machines, while the soldiers of the Wehrmacht had to wait for specialists to repair their broken devices. The democracy of wisdom had a global effect, then. But now, we do not know the culprits who used computers to influence the

2016 U.S. election. They are hidden. The binary priests of the code are like invisible demons who reach down and tweak your brain, then you vote for an idiot, and in voting for an idiot, you become a fool, a toy, a pawn of the priests of the code.

This is how the wisdom changes us and this is how wisdom dies on the clocks. What once was universal becomes private. What once was open becomes secret and arcane.

What is wisdom in the twenty-first century?

I do not know.

Wisdom can be a tool we use to make better lives. Or it can be a private means to control us. My father's wisdom saved the lives of men who worked in dangerous places. His wisdom had a temporal limit, and now, I have to ask, does anyone care anymore about all of us?

Have we lost all sense of the Commons?

The idea of the Commons is more important now than it ever was. As population increases, it taxes resources. Once resources are exhausted, there can be only death and destruction. We need to limit who we are and how many of us there are. This can best be done by choice, which comes from Enlightenment.

As a man, I know that I must rely on women to save the world because the killer in men is still unleashed and will not be put back in its cage for a long, long time.

As I read the news, I am both disgusted and heartened. Disgusted by the self-serving greed but heartened to think that maybe, in the collective wisdom of the political system, there can be justice as the uncontrolled and uncontrollable demagogue is brought to heel.

Mao Zedong writes that power comes from the barrel of a gun.

The real power lies, however, with the collective wisdom of the many when the many choose to exercise it. I am afraid that if we cannot agree on a goal or a system, future demagogues just might escape their ties. A failure to rein in the fascists might be the end to an incredible experiment.

So, what is wisdom?

I have only one answer. It is a line from my poem, "Beckett's Boils."

"I do not know."